GUIDING PRINCIPLES FOR **THE NEW EARLY CHILDHOOD PROFESSIONAL**

BUILDING ON STRENGTH AND COMPETENCE

VALORA WASHINGTON
AND BRENDA GADSON

FOREWORD BY MARCY WHITEBOOK

TEACHERS COLLEGE PRESS

TEACHERS COLLEGE | COLUMBIA UNIVERSITY
NEW YORK AND LONDON

Published by Teachers College Press, 1234 Amsterdam Avenue, New York, NY 10027

Copyright © 2017 by Teachers College, Columbia University

Cover design by adam b. bohannon. Photo by Creativel / iStock by Getty Images.

Library of Congress Cataloging-in-Publication Data is available at loc.gov

ISBN 978-0-8077-5869-4 (paper)
ISBN 978-0-8077-7664-3 (ebook)

Printed on acid-free paper
Manufactured in the United States of America

24 23 22 21 20 19 18 17   8 7 6 5 4 3 2 1

EARLY CHILDHOOD EDUCATION SERIES

SHARON RYAN, EDITOR

To look for other titles in this series, visit www.tcpress.com

continued

To the
420,000 early childhood educators
who have earned a
Child Development Associate Credential

Contents

Foreword

When I began my early childhood career at the beginning of the 1970s, I entered teaching like many of my peers because it allowed me to align my interests in child development with my commitment to working for social justice. The right of all children and families to high-quality, affordable early childhood services provided by highly skilled, well-paid, and supported educators—as I understood then and continue to believe today—holds the promise of reducing the pervasive inequities in the United States that stem from poverty and racial, gender, and class discrimination. But as I soon came to understand and continue to lament, our early childhood system, despite some notable strides, has evolved in such a way that it often reinforces an unequal playing field for children, families, and teachers alike.

In my first job teaching infants and toddlers, and later working with preschoolers, I directly experienced the low value accorded to early childhood practitioners. It didn't take long to find other teachers who shared my experience and concerns. Before the era of evidence-based policy and practice, we took it upon ourselves to document the rampant poverty-level wages, poor working conditions, and inadequate access to education and training endemic to early childhood employment. We recognized that these conditions made it difficult to attract staff, fueled turnover, undermined the quality of services, and impeded efforts to improve and sustain quality. At the time, we assumed that by sharing the facts, remedies would soon be forthcoming.

To our surprise and dismay, our efforts to highlight the working conditions for teachers and their impact on our well-being and practice were met with resistance and disapproval by many in the field. We had failed to understand that many who championed early care and education privileged the needs of children and families over those of their teachers and providers. Many field leaders considered our calls for worthy wages and better working conditions as either antithetical to the professionalization of the field or issues that should be deferred until the profession was more firmly established.

In their latest book, *Guiding Principles for the New Early Childhood Professional: Building on Strength and Competence,* Valora Washington and Brenda Gadson counter this perspective on professionalizing—and what and who it should encompass—by urging us to grapple with questions of social justice as we seek to promote strategies for elevating the profession. Respect for "the people whose works sustains the existence of our field" and acknowledgment of their strengths, the authors assert, must be central to how we leverage opportunities for reform and overcome long-standing challenges. "Architects of change" for our profession, they maintain, must also be "perceivers of truth." These pages are teeming with uncomfortable realities about how social justice concerns are sidelined in conversations about professionalizing the field and how early childhood practitioners are still missing at decisionmaking tables.

The authors' perspective, garnered from their years working directly with practitioners in centers and homes around the country, draws our attention not only to the muted and sometimes absent voice of practitioners but to the lack of respect embodied in how practitioners are viewed, treated, and talked about, even within the field. By articulating principles—Respect, Competence, Strengths, and Equity—to guide our efforts to define the *new early childhood profession*, Washington and Gadson challenge us to consider where we stray from these principles, and provide examples of how we can enact strategies to counter this.

The authors do not shy away from the uncomfortable dynamics operating in the field and emphasize how such dynamics must be transformed from being seen as "undiscussable" to becoming central topics of conversation. They urge us to talk about the power imbalance between field leaders shaping strategies for the field and ECE practitioners, the latter of whom are more likely to be paid hourly, face economic insecurity, have less access to education, and are more likely to be women of color and speak a language other than English.

Culling together facts, stories, and commentaries, Washington and Gadson invite us to examine matters of conscience and ask ourselves whether we are doing the right thing. As in their previous book, their invitation includes a conceptual and practical pathway for engaging in the difficult and necessary work to disrupt the status quo, which increasingly embraces the importance of young children's teachers but still expects early educators to defer necessary rewards and serve as a source of public support through poor compensation in lieu of public investment.

The authors call on all of us to commit to making social justice for early educators a cornerstone of professionalizing the early childhood field, helping us to see that therein lies the power of our profession and our ability to equitably meet the needs of children and families. Throughout their careers, and again in this new book, Washington and Gadson have demonstrated the courage, wisdom, and dedication required of "architects of change."

—Marcy Whitebook

Acknowledgments

We are thankful to the many colleagues in our early childhood education community who have provided us with so much inspiration and guidance.

Because this book stems from our networks with the CAYL Institute (Community Advocates for Young Learners) and with the Council for Professional Recognition, we especially acknowledge all the Fellows and the entire Child Development Associate (CDA) community. Special thanks are due to Kenneth Murphy, the Council's communications executive, and Linda Jackson, a consultant to the Council.

The Council staff and board have our special appreciation. Together we have worked over the past 7 years to strengthen, streamline, and expand the CDA credentials—ensuring that we offer early childhood educators "the best first step" in their professional journeys.

Many early childhood educators shared their stories with us as we prepared this book. We are humbled by their openness and honesty and inspired by their commitment to this work. In this book we share reflections by 21 of these early educators. Our thanks to Maureen Boggs, Mary Beth Bush, Louis Finney, Robert Gundling, Ron Herndon, Kathy Keller, Lori Kelly, Robyn Lightcamp, Kay Lisseck, B. B. Otero, Pamela Perrino, Brenda Powers, Christine Pruitt, Brocklin Qualls, Aisha Ray, Belinda Rojas, Cindy Rojas Rodriquez, Marta Rosa, Daniela Santos, Cecile Tousignant, and Kamilah Washington. This book also presents the stories of individuals who are identified only by their first names to preserve their anonymity. We thank you all!

We further acknowledge the consideration and encouragement that we highly value from Teachers College Press, specifically our editor, Sarah Biondello, and her colleague Erin Bailey.

Finally, we honor our immediate and extended family members for their unwavering love and support. They are our heartbeats. They light up our lives and fill our world with treasures. We know we have been blessed, and we are grateful.

Guiding Change
Let's Talk!

This book articulates the Guiding Principles that we recommend to govern change and changemakers—early childhood educators asking themselves an essential question of conscience: *Are we doing the right thing?* We offer a focus on Respect, Competence, Strengths, and Equity as Guiding Principles to support the strategic advancement of both our profession and the people who work in it.

These Principles emerge from our work with the CAYL Institute which, since 2004, continuously has offered a forum for early childhood educators to ask questions and to seek answers. A basic CAYL (pronounced "kale") Institute premise is that during this dynamic era of interest in early learning, early childhood educators must be better organized, equipped, and empowered to lead change for both children and early childhood educators. In 2015, *The New Early Childhood Professional*[1] was published as a four-path framework for change based on the challenges and concerns, as well as the stories and strategies, of early childhood educators who had participated in CAYL initiatives (see Figure I.1).

These Guiding Principles for change also are informed by Valora Washington's leadership since 2011 of the Council for Professional Recognition and its signature credentialing system, the Child Development Associate (CDA) Credential™. With its focus on the education of children aged birth to 5 years, the Council is the premier national credentialing organization in the early childhood education field in the United States. Between 1985 and 2016, over 420,000 credentials (120,000 during Valora Washington's tenure) have been awarded to early childhood educators who work in infant/toddler, preschool, family child-care, and home visitor settings. The CDA credentials and the Council directly impact the careers of more early childhood educators than any other early childhood organization in the United States.

Today's thought leaders are abuzz with conversation about "professionalizing" and "defining" the field of early childhood education: What roles constitute the field? Who's in and who's out? What do staff in various roles need to know and be able to do? This is good news—and a clear signal that conversations about change are accelerating in directions that the field leaders have encouraged for decades. The question raised by Valora and Stacie Goffin in their 2007 book *Ready or Not* remains relevant: Are we *ready or not?*

While we are engaged and encouraged by all the buzz, we realize that the field has started down these pathways of change many times before. Any change effort inevitably will surface the field's deep issues, challenge our values, generate disruption, and spawn gigantic misunderstandings. Equipping all of us to be more strategic leaders is a prime purpose of our 2015 "step-by-step guide to overcoming Goliath" ("Goliath" represents all the persistent and daunting challenges that our field and our workforce face—challenges that the Guiding Principles of Respect, Competence, Strengths, and Equity help us to overcome).

Figure I.1. Eleven Interconnected Steps Toward Becoming an Architect of Change

ANALYZE!—Think and Reflect

Step 1: Reality—Face It! We must be honest and contemplative about the challenges and capacities that represent the contest that lies before us.

Step 2: Respect Our Knowledge. We know more than we think we do! We have yet to bring the full power of our knowledge to bear in our work.

ADVANCE!—Plan and Prepare

Step 3: Recognize Symptoms of Asymmetrical Conflict. We need to recognize the factors of isolation, intimidation, and negation when they occur.

Step 4: Reassess Your Willingness to Face Goliath. Now comes the critical decision: advance or retreat?

Step 5: Revelation—Know Your Vision and Identity. To realize our vision, we must affiliate, belong, and connect to one another and to our profession.

ACT!—Be Brave and Bold

Step 6: Join a Confidential Community and Share Leadership. As we strive for personal mastery, each of us must share strategies and encourage one another.

Step 7: Begin with Your Everyday Challenges. Think about the issues that you face every day. This is the place where you begin your work.

Step 8: Align What We Know with What We Do. We must use what we know every day, in every situation, in every interaction with a child, parent, peer, or administrator.

ACCELERATE!—Believe and Achieve

Step 9: Focus on What You Do Want, Not What You Don't Want. Too often we worry away our hours and days thinking about the negative, and focus on what we don't want to happen.

Step 10: Don't Walk Alone—Gather Your Allies. It is simply unwise to walk up to Goliath and face him down without colleagues, friends, and supervisors.

Step 11: Get the Word Out—Document and Communicate Impact. Just as the story of David and Goliath is part of our shared mythology and heritage, our stories as early educators must be recorded for future generations.

THE URGENT QUEST TO PROFESSIONALIZE

At no time in history has the imperative to professionalize the early childhood education workforce been greater. A resounding sense of urgency emerges from an incontrovertible body of evidence and insight about the critical period of birth to age 5 for both child development and learning. The Institute of Medicine (IOM) and the National Research Council (NRC)[2] summarize this evidence as follows:

- the neuroscience of brain development
- research demonstrating the profound long-term effects of high-quality early learning
- economic analysis on the societal benefits of investing in young children
- greater clarity about the impact of teacher behavior on child outcomes

One result of this new knowledge is the rapid growth of the field of early childhood education—the workforce is large, comprising about 1 million persons working in center-based programs, and another 1 million paid home-based workers.[3] Another result is that the gap between what we know and what we do for young children is becoming more visible: Early childhood education is not as well developed in the United States as in some other countries; the United States ranks about 28th in the percentage of 4-year-olds in early childhood education, with a 69% enrollment rate.[4] And there is a clear need to increase the quality of early childhood education for all children, since high quality is still too rare.[5] Consequently, the field is in the midst of a major historical shift from a relatively low public profile to a policy focus that demands increased accountability and high-quality results for young children.

But professionalizing the field is a complex challenge complicated by the field's lack of clarity about its purpose, identity, and responsibilities. To professionalize, the field—and the society in which it is embedded—must grapple with thorny topics such as stable financing, workforce qualifications, facility management, governance systems, program standards, and public expectations. Progress in any of these topics has the potential to stimulate breakthroughs in decades of deadlock about how, and by whom, children under age 5 should be cared for and educated.

As change efforts move forward, these Guiding Principles are both a recognition of a major opportunity for constructive change and a caution of potential obstacles to change: How can we demonstrate respect for the people who actually work with children and families every day? To what extent will practicing early childhood educators be represented in the important conversations about change? How can we identify aspects of the field's culture that should be preserved? Will we—and how *can* we—minimize the unintended consequences of change? The change agent—the new early childhood professional—must never fail to ask: Are we doing the right thing? And, are we doing the right thing for *all children?*

We continually ask this question because, with decades of experience working in this field, we are deeply invested in it. We recognize in our colleagues deep and unwavering wells of passion, good will, courage, and commitment to social justice for both children and their families.

Moreover, the ideals of inclusion and innovation are evergreen for us. And we, as the authors, have benefited from our hands-on direct experiences with the careers of thousands of practitioners. We are compelled to give back by sharing lessons learned from their dreams, hopes, and fears about change. These Guiding Principles reflect what we have learned through the privilege of these relationships.

The critical message is this: The effectiveness of the field's change strategies *requires* each of us to elevate the voices of the early childhood education practitioner. "Power to our profession" *demands* leadership from the rank and file as well as from national and state thought leaders. Ensuring a better future for young children and their families cannot happen without *active consent* of the forces within the nursery, the home-based business, the classroom, and the school. And, as we focus on change, we must identify and build on our core strengths, not just "fix" what is wrong.

We encourage you to read these Guiding Principles with an open mind, understanding that the experiences of some early childhood education professionals from the practice floor or the policy landscape sometimes might seem odd, confusing, painful, and even false to other professionals. To become an architect of change is also to become a perceiver of multiple truths, knowing that our focus must be, and must always remain, first and foremost, on serving *people,* not proving them wrong. Building our capacity to listen and learn builds trust and ultimately creates a source of power for our profession.

So, let's talk as we welcome, embrace, and pursue change!

TRUTHS, DILEMMAS, AND CONTRADICTIONS

Stacie Goffin and Valora Washington identified three defining issues believed to be central to the field's leadership work:

1. What is the field's defining intent or *purpose*?
2. For what is the field willing to be responsible?
3. What is the field's *identity* or distinctive contribution and competence as a collective entity?

At the core, these remain the salient questions that many contemporary change efforts seek to address. This is often what is meant by efforts to "define" the field and who should be a member of it.

Let's start with a fundamental question: *What defines an early childhood educator?*

We offer the following definition of the early childhood educator, only partly tongue-in-cheek, because we believe our definition illustrates the need for Guiding Principles as practitioners, advocates, and thought leaders grapple with "who's in and who's out" of the field:

> **Early childhood educator** (noun): Person whose profession is highly valued, of deferred value, and undervalued all at once!

By this definition, multiple peculiar truths, dilemmas, and contradictions are immediately evident.

- It is true that *early childhood educators are people whose profession is highly valued for its capacity to build human capital*. The public, we believe, now understands that the early years are critical learning years that have long-lasting social and economic impacts on children, their families, and society as a whole.
- This truth unmasks a dilemma—a situation in which a difficult undesirable choice is made: The vigor with which public actors *celebrate* the science of early learning does not yet equal the vigor with which public actors *invest* in the people who bring that science to life. Consequently, *early childhood educators are also people whose profession requires them to offer themselves as a* source *of*

DEFINITIONS

We acknowledge that the field of early childhood education (ECE) is defined as birth through age 8. In this book, however, references to the workforce focus primarily on those who serve children prior to kindergarten. Workforce issues for school-aged children typically have different norms, working conditions, compensation structures, and contexts.

public support while the nation defers decisions about appropriate levels of public investment. The "deferral" gap between public acclaim and public investment is reflected in the compensation and working conditions of many practitioners.

- The deferral gap also supports a pervasive contradiction—a combination of ideas, or features of a situation, that are opposed to one another. Despite the science,[6] the economics,[7] and the educational "power"[8] that the field of early childhood education can deliver for children, families, and our nation, the undeniable fact remains that early childhood educators themselves continually are maligned by misconceptions that this career requires minimal knowledge, competencies, and skills. *Early childhood educators are people who work in a profession so undervalued and undermined that it is often wrongly considered to be a synonym of a role called "babysitting."* We discourage language that equates early childhood education with babysitting. Similarly, we discourage the use of the term "day care," which conjures images of babysitting rather than structured and enriching early learning programs. Early childhood educators care for children, not days.

It is astonishing that these three highly unharmonious definitions of the early childhood professional could exist simultaneously—but they do! These are head-spinning, peculiar truths, dilemmas, and contradictions. This situation explains why *The New Early Childhood Professional* uses the analogy of David and Goliath[9] to express the isolation, negation, and intimidation early childhood educators often feel because they are confronted with seemingly insurmountable stereotypes.

These varied and simultaneously held views about early childhood educators are not benign; they pose a triple threat. They threaten our:

- ability to serve young children fully and well
- capacity to advance as a profession
- nation's economic future

Yet, in the midst of these circumstances, by any definition of the field, generations of early childhood educators have continued to advance the field with passion, persistence, and grit; they do so by demonstrating love, eliciting trust from families, and expressing a commitment to change. As difficult choices about the field's identity are grappled with, conversations about "who's in and who's out" should be influenced by the Guiding Principle of demonstrating respect for the people whose life's work sustains the existence of our field.

FACING GOLIATH

For the field of early childhood education, change is not optional. The question is not whether we change, or whether, for example, we courageously seek more coherent definitions of the field. The question is how we best prepare to be architects of that change rather than passive recipients of it, and how we manage change rather than become entrapped in historical bugaboos that become "undiscussables."[10]

This is a significant undertaking.

As in the well-known story of David and Goliath, who among us has not felt the quiet despair of feeling weak in the face of the strong? But today, in an era of escalating hopes,[11] there are opportunities to fulfill the deferred promises of early childhood education for both young children and early childhood educators.

Collaborating about change is challenging—even more so in a profession long accustomed to the one-off autonomy that indeed yielded great creativity and variety within the profession largely because it often was publicly ignored. Our focus now must be on the *collective* challenges of the field, with a strategic emphasis on building professional communities, strengthening our professional capital, and working together to craft solutions.

The solutions will not necessarily be clear-cut, or easily won. At the time of this writing, there are several national "field-defining" collaboratives underway (including Power to the Profession and a workgroup organized by the National Academy of Medicine),[12] each of which has gathered representatives from national organizations. We support and participate in these collaboratives, and value the commitment of the individuals who give their time to such efforts wherever they occur. The Guiding Principles will support the excellence of our work together.

ESSENTIAL COMPANIONS

The 2 million[13] early childhood educators in the United States cannot literally sit together over several years to define a profession. It is nevertheless essential that field-defining strategies give voice to the aspirations and expressions of the many early childhood educators who are not present in the important local, state, and national dialogues taking place about change.

Always remember that the 2 million not present are our essential companions because, unlike many leaders of national organizations that think and write about this field, these essential companions may be more likely to possess the following characteristics:

- Have or have had actual work experience with children and families
- Be an hourly employee with few or no benefits
- Speak a language other than English
- Be a person of color
- Be low income and a recipient of public assistance
- Have few academic degrees and limited access to higher education

These characteristics and experiences add significant value to our thinking about how to define and advance the field. We must recognize—but neither minimize nor magnify—the realities of our workforce in the present era. The Guiding Principles urge us not to proceed without a diversity of voices. This diversity of occupational experiences matters enormously because they represent multiple truths, and truth is only as powerful as the trust we have in those who speak it. We are ill advised to pretend that these realities do not exist—or to allow them to remain or become "undiscussable."

What all of us in the field of early childhood education have in common is an earnest desire for a clearer vision of a unified future in early childhood education. A leadership challenge is to anticipate difference, facilitate difficult dialogue, and create spaces where *asymmetrical conflict* (the recognition that power is imbalanced) can be voiced, discussed, and acted upon.

LEADERSHIP DILEMMAS

Enhancing the professional stature of the early childhood education field requires an enormous bounty of good will and trust. On the one hand, professionalizing the field is, virtually, a universally endorsed idea. On the other hand, the strategic priorities, implementation decisions, and messaging that sometimes accompany "professionalization" have not always been universally experienced in the same way. Here are a few examples:

ASYMMETRICAL CONFLICT

We are adapting the term *asymmetrical conflict* to describe the relative inequalities and disadvantages faced by the early childhood educator as well as by young children in our society. The exercise of power is experienced indirectly as well as through imbalanced distribution of services and resources. The concept of asymmetrical conflict has a fuller discussion in *The New Early Childhood Professional* by Washington, Gadson, and Amel.

- Rapid change in program and practitioner requirements can be "received" as messages that the staff are not "good enough" (Chapter 1, Respect)
- The advantages of degree attainment are not always perceived in on-the-ground implementation (Chapter 2, Competence)
- "Fixing" the field can lend itself to a deficit paradigm, rather than a Strengths approach to our workforce and our work (Chapter 3, Strengths)
- The voices and concerns of people of color are under-represented (Chapter 4, Equity)

To be sure, we believe that differential outcomes of professionalization efforts can be unintended consequences—and not deliberate snubs. In this book, we name these dilemmas of professionalization, even as we realize that some colleagues might rush to deny that these perspectives are "real." Our commitment to the field of early childhood education compels us to name these dilemmas because we cannot change what we cannot face. Guiding Principles focus our attention on the need to have respect for diverse opinions, to seek equity, and to acknowledge the field's strengths, while doing the challenging work to enhance competence.

FOUNDATIONS FOR GUIDING PRINCIPLES

Guiding Principles are an important preamble to, and facilitator of, strategic change. Principles become a vital conceptual framework and grounding with which to approach difficult dialogue. We find several resources useful.

Both CAYL and the Council for Professional Recognition adopted Don Miguel Ruiz's 1997 book *The Four Agreements* as a starting point. *The Four Agreements* establishes a strong conceptual framework for approaching personal and professional life:

Agreement 1: Be impeccable with your word. Speak with integrity.
Agreement 2: Don't take anything personally. What other people say has nothing to do with you.
Agreement 3: Don't make assumptions. Ask questions with courage and integrity.
Agreement 4: Always do your best!

The Council staff also uses *The Speed of Trust*[14] by Stephen M. R. Covey. This book articulates 13 behaviors common to high-trust leaders. *The Speed of Trust* centers on the idea that the ability to establish, extend, and restore trust is a key leadership competency. More than a soft skill or social virtue, trust impacts business results and is a performance multiplier.

THE GUIDING PRINCIPLES

The Guiding Principles enable us both to anticipate "multiple truths" in advance of our collaborative work and to ameliorate and address issues as they occur. Naming Guiding Principles is important to leading change because if we do not define our beliefs and circumstances, misunderstandings are sure to arise that will define these ideas for us. By taking ownership of our own values and defining what's important to us, we establish a foundation that will shepherd us through the rough waters of leading change.

Guiding Principles describe our change strategy beliefs and philosophy. They should direct what our change strategy intends to do, why it needs to be done, and how we plan to achieve the changes. These Guiding Principles (see Figure I.2) are intended to support each and all of us as we design and implement any change strategy throughout the life of the initiative, regardless of possible changes in the leadership or focus of the work.

Throughout this book, we capitalize each of the four Guiding Principles as a way to emphasize them. For each of the four Guiding Principles—Respect, Competence, Strengths, and Equity—we use the following six-part format:

1. We *define* the Principle. For example: What does the Principle of Competence mean and how does it impact individual practitioners, early childhood programs, public policies, and professional systems?
2. We identify potential *asymmetrical conflicts* related to the Principle, to demonstrate the imbalances that exist.
3. We present *voices* from the field. The book presents the real stories of members of the early childhood field. (In a few cases, individuals in this book are identified only by their first names to preserve their anonymity.)
4. We sum up each chapter with a "bottom-line" analysis that we call *Achieving Balance*. These are "must add" ideas to the field's approach to change.
5. We present affirmations for *Facing Goliath*—short, intentional, and powerful statements of belief. These affirmations emphasize the truths we want to create in order to accelerate the emergence of a new reality for the field. We offer these affirmations with love, faith, and intention. What we think about our challenges is what we will create!
6. We offer opportunities to *Reflect* on each Guiding Principle. At the end of each chapter we offer questions to help you relate that Principle to your own circumstances.

Figure I.2. Guiding Principles to Lead Change for the Early Childhood Education Profession

Principle	Definition	Asymmetrical Conflict	Practitioner Voice	Facing Goliath	Achieving Balance
Respect	Acknowledge and demonstrate absolute dignity for practitioners	Practitioners experience widespread poverty and low professional status, and may be subject to contempt by some of the field's leaders	"Honor and Respect where people are" —Robert Gundling "Respect can't be separated from Equity" —Pam Perrino	Early childhood educators make valuable contributions, and deserve a safe and productive work environment, economic security, and professional recognition	Professionalizing the field should focus on professional capital rather than individual worker shortcomings. It is unethical to keep asking the practitioner to "wait" for change
Competence	Define the observable and measurable behaviors or characteristics that articulate the field's distinctive contributions	The field emphasizes degree acquisition without consensus about what the practitioner should know and be able to do	"Teachers need both knowledge and practical experience" —Louis Finney	Degree attainment is an insufficient proxy for Competence in ECE	We must build ECE teacher education as a challenging discipline using communities of practice and a new vision for higher education
Strengths	Decide what is essential to retain and bring forward—and map and preserve its assets	Academic pressures on teaching suppress recognition that soft skills and intangibles drive performance!	"Children are not going to learn unless there is a relationship with that teacher" —Cecile Tousignant	The field's growing focus on degree attainment and test results must never overcome the value of love, trust, commitment, and relationships in work with children and families	As professional mastery increases, the soft skills may matter more than ever in practitioner performance.
Equity	Address disparities, exercise power with others, protect the rights of our colleagues, and serve as an instrument of professional cohesion	Some efforts to professionalize the field can exacerbate inequities between program and practitioners	"We do not train teachers to actually know what to do about culture except through the most superficial ways . . . I don't think you can get significant advantages and change for kids of color unless you begin to change who is in the pipeline to make the policy." —Aisha Ray	The field must address the demonstrated failure of the market economy for child care, the lack of representative leadership among the field's leaders, as well as racial and gender discrimination	Professionalizing the field must include a focus on Equity and social justice. We must be "willing to be disturbed" —Margaret Wheatley

OUR HOPES FOR OUR READERS

These four Guiding Principles and the issues that underlie the need for them must now be considered with a greater sense of urgency. We have four major hopes for this book:

1. We hope that *Guiding Principles for the New Early Childhood Professional* will increase your sense of Respect for the dignity, value, and professionalism of the front-line practitioner.
2. We hope that, because of the Guiding Principles, you will have greater awareness of the need for field-defining competencies, recognizing that degree attainment is only a proxy for this indicator of a profession.
3. We hope that the Guiding Principles will inspire your appreciation for the soft skills and intangibles that drive professional performance.
4. We hope that the Guiding Principles will strengthen your willingness to be uncomfortable as we tackle the complex realities practitioners face as we strive for Equity.

LET'S TALK!

As change agents, we want to answer affirmatively when reflecting on the question, "Are we doing the right thing?" Let's continue to talk as we welcome, embrace, and pursue change! We trust that these Guiding Principles will help our profession to become stronger, more effective, and more authentically supported and appreciated.

CHAPTER 1

Respect!

From the Latin *respicere*, which means "to consider," "to look back at," and "to look again."

Respect for children, families, and colleagues is a core value in the code of ethical conduct of the National Association for the Education of Young Children (NAEYC).[1] But let's look again: What is Respect? And why does it need to be called out as a Guiding Principle for the new early childhood professional?

WHAT IS RESPECT?

Respect is often difficult to define. But each of us clearly senses when we feel respected—or do not.

Much of our everyday thinking about Respect is derived from an 18th-century German philosopher, Immanuel Kant. Kant was among the first Western philosophers to put Respect for persons at the very center of moral law and to insist that persons are ends unto themselves with an absolute dignity.[2] In the modern world, the notion of Respect for persons typically means that people are owed Respect just because they are persons, regardless of their social position, individual characteristics, achievements, or moral merit. Indeed, in our democratic society, Respect for all persons is a basic ideology.

Respect is a valuable asset in the workplace, yet over half of employees around the world indicate that they don't regularly get Respect from their leaders. Employees say that being treated with Respect is more important to them than recognition and appreciation, communicating an inspiring vision, providing useful feedback—even opportunities for learning, growth, and development.[3] Even witnessing, but not directly experiencing, incivility in the workplace can cause performance to drop by half.[4] This reaction is to be expected because, in contemporary culture, it commonly is understood that, at some level, everyone is worthy of Respect.

The person who respects something, pays attention to it. The idea of giving attention to someone implies seeing the person clearly in his or her own right. When we Respect people, we are not oblivious to them, nor do we ignore, dismiss, neglect, discount, degrade, or disregard them. We do not carelessly or intentionally misidentify them.[5]

How might Respect be understood in the context of the early childhood education profession today? What attitudes and behaviors indicate Respect for early childhood educators—or the lack of it?

A DEFICIT APPROACH?

This basic question of Respect crystallized for Valora Washington several years ago while attending an invitational gathering of about 20 thought leaders convened to brainstorm next steps for the field. She, among a few others, was amazed that the conversation quickly turned to how "they" (current teaching staff) are holding "us" (the field) back from our efforts to raise the quality and reputation of our profession. An array of contemptuous remarks filled the room: "They" are poorly educated, have insufficient vocabularies, are unacquainted with the field's knowledge base, and don't help children achieve the results that we know from research are possible. Unstated but unmistakable was that "they" should be like "us." Yet in that room, the collective "we" had virtually no teaching experience with young children, were composed of almost exclusively White women with graduate degrees, were monolingual English-speaking, and typically were attending the meeting at the expense of our organizations.

In this remarkable moment, the author realized that practitioners are caught in a vise of disrespect from a public that may still think of them as babysitters and from some thought leaders who view them through a deficit lens.

IRONIES OF ASYMMETRICAL POWER

Let us consider and look again at the question of Respect for the early childhood educator.

One irony is that the field for many decades has acted decisively to shift thinking about children and families from a deficit approach to a Strengths-based approach. Yet, the strident efforts with which we promote this paradigm for children are not always extended to the adults who work with them.

Another irony is that so little Respect is rendered to the professionals who are themselves so deeply immersed in demonstrating Respect for the children and families we serve. Respect is a fundamental intention of developmentally appropriate practice for working with infants, toddlers, and pre-schoolers: We demonstrate the importance of Respect for children by listening to them, supporting them to express their views, taking their views into account, involving them in decisionmaking processes, and sharing power with them.[6] As a profession we have a "partic-ipative" ethos in working with young children that conveys a sense of belonging, equality, and active participation. Shouldn't the same ethos be practiced with front-line staff?

Often disrespect is an unintended or un-reflective expression of asymmetrical power of one group toward another, even within the early childhood education field. Certainly, no person or group in the early childhood ed-ucation profession sets out to disregard or degrade the hands-on practitioner, or the sector of the field that one may feel is low-er on the occupational hierarchy than one's own sector.

Rather, the dilemma of disrespect is in it-self a symbol of the field's lack of clarity and insecurity about its professional status. In whatever role we serve the field, we notice the incongruity of a public that is now convinced of the value of early childhood education[7] yet tolerates widespread poverty and limited opportunity among the people who provide that education. The Guiding Principle of Respect reminds us of a vital reality: If anyone in the general public "misidentifies" the infant teacher as a babysitter, the entire field is diminished.

> Education seems to be run from a deficit model. We look at and identify gaps, but successful businesses don't run from a deficit model. They use an asset model. They look at and find the assets of their people, and they grow those assets knowing that someone's deficits will never be their Strengths. Whatever model we choose, we shouldn't start out by identifying gaps but by identifying where our assets are and build upon them.
>
> —Pamela Perrino
> from Ohio

> I recently attended a collaborative group meeting. The group had decided to send a survey out about early childhood needs in the community. The survey was supposed to be sent out to all educators and parents. The survey results had come in and were being discussed. I indicated that there didn't appear to be any community child-care staff among the respondents. I asked who received this survey. The answer was that non–public school providers/personnel were not included in the survey. They obviously didn't consider family child-care providers and child-care center personnel as educators or that their thoughts were important to the process.
>
> —Maureen Boggs from Ohio

The Guiding Principle of Respect draws attention to the need for consciousness about professional hierarchies, occupational privilege, scornful attitudes, and unreflective behaviors as we work to professionalize the field. The strategic objective may be that professionalization will engender greater Respect for our field. Yet the messy reality of implementing new ideas is that, too often—unintentionally perhaps but clearly unmistakably—staff may perceive a startling new message: "You're not good enough to be the new early childhood professional." Therein lays the dilemma of demonstrating Respect.

Consider this: The "staff" are not a threat to professionalism. Rather, their collective Competence is a *symptom* of systemic, asymmetrical challenges and predicaments of the field as a whole. For the most part, the system has failed these teachers—they have not failed the profession. The field's fundamental shortcomings result from complex structural perils, not individual deficits.

Indeed, Respect for practitioners *is* professional. "They" are colleagues who care about the work and who can give their own rational consent for change. "They" are not merely useful or objectified toward ends established by others. "They" are our colleagues to whom we might show Respect and with whom we might reason and collaborate as we work together to elevate the voices of all early childhood education professionals.

RESPECT: ELEPHANTS IN THE ROOM

Professionalizing the field requires multiple and complex strategies, some of which are *external* to the field's direct sphere of influence. Child-care financing, for example, involves an array of complex asymmetrical challenges—political, policy, economic, and societal choices—that have been tackled by generations of child advocates.[8]

> We really need to look at how we get past the perception that we play with young children all day. It's perceived as easy work. The perception isn't about the training, the knowledge, the experience, or what it takes to really educate and teach young children. Our work—it isn't valued or understood.
>
> —Lori Kelly from Ohio

> We have a situation in which my classroom at the YMCA gets additional resources, curriculum support, and compensation because we are part of a special project with Boston Public Schools. This creates tension because the classroom right next door doing the same job doesn't get what we get. This causes resentment among some staff . . . and it's unfair to children who don't have the advantages.
>
> —Kamilah Washington from Massachusetts

On the other hand, there are many aspects of professionalizing the field that can be more immediately influenced or defined by the field itself, such as scholarships, workforce qualifications, licensing standards, and curriculum frameworks. A focus on these types of change initiatives is both a practical and strategic consideration because they lend themselves to real-time funding embellishments and respond to our knowledge base and research.

> There is a culture among decisionmakers and system builders that totally dismisses nondegree people as not having much to offer. I think that sentiment is the norm.
>
> —Maureen Boggs from Ohio

Clearly, many leaders in this field understand that the current strategic emphasis on program quality improvements and a highly qualified workforce does not represent *everything* that is required in order to advance the early childhood education profession. Nevertheless, a lack of field-wide communication structures may lead some practitioners to hear:

- heavy promotion of degree attainment with potential loss of employment if the degree is not attained
- an escalating collection of mandates, directives, and requirements from employers, governments, and associations

Collectively, these massive changes can create a field of practice in which both the practitioners and program directors feel increasingly under siege and disrespected. Are practitioners merely means to ends that they had no role in determining?

RADIO SILENCE

Practitioners clearly are getting the message: Do more. Be more. However, they do not hear about or see much realized change in the issues that impact their daily work lives, such as:

- compensation
- working conditions
- low occupational status

Randi Wolfe states: "Unfortunately, what is clear is that inadequate compensation and lack of workplace supports persist as the greatest challenge and the 'elephant in the room' that is not being directly addressed."[9]

Harriet Dicter, Lea Austin, and Fran Kipnis state:

While the current policy framework and discussion in the states is increasingly focused on delivering quality to young children, and ensuring improved school readiness outcomes, teacher quality is defined primarily in terms of acquisition of degrees, credentials and training. An implicit assumption across state and federal policies, with few exceptions, is that professional salaries will follow increases in education and credential levels. As a result, the task of creating intentional policies to address compensation is generally ignored. Of the five out of ten National Institute for Early Education Research (NIEER) benchmarks of high-quality state preschool programs that address teaching staff, all are focused on teacher qualifications; compensation is not included."[10]

Whitebook, McLean, and Austin point out:

Compensation and retention are important markers of quality . . . [but only] eighteen states include salary scales and/or benefit options, such as health insurance and paid leave from work, as benchmarks of program quality for center-based programs, while only about half as many include this indicator for home-based providers.[11]

Those authors further note:

Improvements to policies and resources that address teachers' economic well-being have been largely optional, selective, and sporadic. They have not translated evenly to federal policy or funding priorities across programs, nor have they necessarily prompted state actions. A major goal of early childhood services has been to relieve poverty among children, yet many of these same efforts continue to generate poverty in the predominantly female, ethnically and racially diverse ECE workforce, especially for educators who have children of their own.[12]

"Radio silence" (a period during which one hears nothing from a normally communicative person or group) can be interpreted as disrespect. In the absence of *equally visible* pursuits of additional strategic priorities, "deficits" in the early childhood education workforce are illuminated and magnified. It can sound like: You're

> Respect comes from the top. I feel strongly that it starts with the leaders and administrators of programs. It is part of their job to help staff feel professional and respected. We must support leaders in nurturing and communicating the value of the profession to their staff so they can feel better about the job they do. Leaders must be better prepared to communicate the value of the work and to support, develop, and elevate their staff.
>
> —Kathy Keller from Texas

not good enough to earn a living wage. A college degree will make you better, so earn that degree as fast as you can so we can professionalize the field.

TAKING A DIFFERENT PERSPECTIVE

Yes! Professionalizing the field matters, unquestionably. But there are social contexts, multiple truths, and critical questions that deserve parity in our conversation about strategic priorities. Here are three contextual questions related to the issue of balancing respectful discourse:

- *Who wants to be a teacher?* We live in an era where the entire profession of teaching is under pressure as fewer adults choose this career path.[13] Teacher shortages are becoming a real problem—but there is no shortage of critiques about the teaching profession.[14] Early childhood educators are not isolated from this phenomenon.
- *Who wants to stay poor?* A "highly qualified early childhood education workforce" is not necessarily the workforce that program directors can afford to pay or retain. Many directors report to us that they cannot find staff at all, never mind those with a bachelor's degree.
- *Who will "stay put" as the profession disrupts, changes, and grows?* Decades of effort in the field have hardly budged the poverty-level wages.[15] So it comes as no surprise that, as early childhood educators achieve a bachelor's degree, they sometimes use that degree to find more lucrative employment (to the chagrin of strategists working diligently to professionalize the field with this approach).[16]

Early childhood educators can—and do—vote with their feet in a decades-long phenomenon called "turnover."[17] Yet, we are amazed by how many are committed to *staying* in the field, often at great personal sacrifice, because of their desire to make a difference in the lives of young children and their families. These dedicated teachers recognize the unrealized power of our profession. They deserve our Respect.

RESPECTFUL LISTENING

There are many ways to demonstrate Respect when implementing or embracing new change strategies. Balancing new occupational requirements with respectful listening would include:

- truly seeing the world from the practitioners' point of view
- appreciating, promoting, and protecting practitioners' values when those values may be different from our own
- helping them to pursue their ends
- recognizing and preserving their assets (see Chapter 3 on Strengths)

Kant's work suggests that although members of the early childhood education community may or may not have meritorious accomplishments,

---

PROFILE OF PAMELA PERRINO,
EARLY CHILDHOOD ADVOCATE AND EDUCATIONAL CONSULTANT

As someone who works with leaders and professionals from across the early childhood education landscape—family child-care providers, centers, and school-based pre-K programs—Pamela Perrino understands what it takes to build Respect among people from these different settings, as well as how easily it can be torn down.

"Throwing money at collaboration is not always the best incentive," says Perrino, who works in Trumbull County, Ohio. "I have seen at the local level that as soon as the money goes away, so does the collaboration if trust, mutual Respect, and mission have not been established."

Too often, she says, people are driven by an agenda and time constraints and don't take time to get to know those that they are supposed to be collaborating with.

"There is a happy medium if you build relationships and trust," she says. "When they come together to hurry up and get this done, there is a lot of scar tissue that's left behind."

When Perrino is on conference calls or in meetings with those who represent different types of early learning programs, she tries to be "intentional about drawing them out of their comfort zone" and making sure they are heard. But she adds that one major obstacle is that gatherings sometimes are scheduled when at-home or center-based providers can't attend because they can't afford to hire substitutes.

"How can you be at the table to garner Respect and knowledge if you're not equitably funded to be there?" she asks.

Respect, she adds, can't be separated from Equity, and when programs have to compete against one another for funding, working together to meet the needs of children and families becomes more difficult. One example, she says, is the expansion of public, school-based preschool.

"It's not a delivery system that meets families' needs," she says. "Families need 52 weeks a year, evenings and weekends."

and may have or lack "evaluative" Respect, all persons as members of the community are owed "recognition" Respect. People should never be treated as means to our ends, as if their only value were what derives from their usefulness to us. Their dignity should never be degraded or forfeited. It is important to remember that the field will professionalize to the extent that we recognize teacher needs that extend beyond professional development. We professionalize the field *and* honor staff when quality improvement efforts highlight what teachers need, in addition to training and education, to help children succeed.

OPPORTUNITY, PATHWAYS, AND RECOGNITION

In addition to compensation parity, practitioners want opportunities to do their best work, practical career pathways, and professional recognition.

Opportunity

Early childhood educators have a strong sense that what they do matters; what they do serves something larger than their immediate self-interest. They want opportunities to do their best work, the resources to serve children's individual needs, and an understanding of the community contexts in which their work is performed.

> The worst part is that we don't get the support we need to work with children who have special needs for mental health support. Some of these children are traumatized by their life situations and environments. We would like more opportunities to take children to cultural institutions such as the children's museum. We teachers speak out about it but nothing seems to change.
>
> —Kamilah Washington from Massachusetts

Practitioners can do their best work when the realities of their daily work are recognized and addressed. For example, the world of working with young children is a world in which one's attention constantly is drawn in many directions. It is practically the definition of multitasking. Yet, practitioners have few opportunities or encouragement to intermittently rest and renew their energy during the work day. Many feel overloaded when dealing with the intense and relentless physical demands of working with young children.

Planning time also would make it possible for practitioners to work at a higher level of quality.

> Paid time for teachers to plan or prepare for children's activities is essential to a high-quality service, but it is not a guarantee for early childhood educators, many of whom must plan while simultaneously caring for children or during unpaid hours.[18]

Pathways

Opportunities to do their best work for children also are closely tied to learning opportunities for practitioners themselves. Although there are numerous promising pilot projects and many exceptional leaders who work for change, access to coherent channels for professional mobility has not emerged on a field-wide basis.

Let us take a comparative look: When students enter a nursing program, there is a standard body of knowledge that their training will cover and a set of skills they will acquire. The same holds true for many other professions.

But those who are studying to be early childhood educators don't necessarily have the assurance that the courses or training in which they are participating will prepare them adequately for teaching and caring for young children. This is an age-old challenge in the early childhood education field (and is one of the reasons the Child Development Associate Credential™ was created for entry-level professionals over 40 years ago).

As a result of these circumstances, even the most strongly motivated practitioners seeking higher education can experience immense difficulty in creating, finding, completing, and financing a career pathway in early childhood education. This situation is even more arduous for English language learners, a fast-growing component of the workforce.[19]

Recognition

The spectacular progress of the field in attaining a growing proportion of credentialed staff is even more astonishing given the field's lack of coherence about workforce qualifications. This success is even more gratifying because we know that many early childhood educators—adult learners who are employed, studying, and taking care of family responsibilities—take longer to matriculate.

It is in this context that the recognition of multiple truths and perspectives becomes an important matter of Respect. Marcy Whitebook and her colleagues found that faculty viewed these adults as "stalled" due to the length of time it takes to achieve their academic goals, while the students' self-perceptions were that they were "making progress in a realistic and appropriate way due to their life situations."[20]

Making judgments about the workforce without walking in their shoes is an indicator of a point made earlier: The reality experienced by early childhood education professionals from the practice floor and from the university classroom may be different, but one is not more valid than the other. As the field professionalizes, we must acknowledge multiple truths, knowing that our focus must be, and must always remain, first and foremost on serving *people*, not proving them wrong.

PROFILE OF MARYBETH BUSH, OWNER/OPERATOR, MARY'S LITTLE LAMBS CHILD CARE AND PRESCHOOL

When the H.A.P.P.Y Homes association for family child-care providers formed in Trumbull County, Ohio, almost 20 years ago, there were about 200 licensed providers in the area. Now MaryBeth Bush, one of the organizers of the group—an affiliate of the National Association for Family Child Care— has seen that number dwindle down to about 40.

"Right now is a tough time for family providers," says Bush. Not only are regulations for at-home providers getting tougher to meet, but many providers, she says, are leaving the profession because they think they can't meet the standards set by the state's Step Up to Quality rating system. "Even though I thought they could do it, they didn't think they could."

The declining supply, Bush says, also leaves many parents with fewer choices. Because only three of the six children she is licensed to care for can be infants, she often has to refer families to other providers. "I have nothing against centers," she says, "but I have a really hard time referring someone to a center for an infant."

She also sees parents opting for unlicensed providers and care by relatives when they can't find regulated homes.

A mentor to other family child-care providers, Bush grew up taking care of her younger siblings as well as the many infants her parents fostered until they were adopted. After working at restaurants and then having her second child, Bush knew that she wanted to stay home and care for children. She was part of an initial cohort in the state to earn a CDA. Then she completed an associate's degree and is only a few courses away from earning a bachelor's degree through the University of Cincinnati's online program.

Bush works to form connections with center-based providers, pre-K and kindergarten teachers, and early childhood advocates in the area, and makes sure that family child care is well represented in conversations about improving early education.

"They get to hear what family child care is about," she says, adding that her program provides an environment for children that many parents prefer. "Parents come here because they want child care that feels like a home."

Respect can mean *refraining* from regarding or treating practitioners in certain ways. With respect to practitioners we ought not:

- disregard their viewpoints or experiences as "less than" those of others
- show contempt for them
- ridicule, mock, coerce, or deceive them

According to Porath, the real reason leaders fail to act respectfully is a lack of self-awareness. "More often people just do not realize how they affect others," these authors write in the *Harvard Business Review*. "They may have good intentions, but they fail to see how they are perceived."[21]

Respect means that these early childhood educators will be valued and recognized for their accomplishments, creating a deeper level of trust and security in our field of practice. With Respect, practitioners can spend less energy seeking and defending their value, and more energy creating it.[22]

Here are just a few observations worthy of respectful recognition:

- Practitioners are achieving higher levels of academic qualifications faster than the state requirements for such qualifications (see Chapter 2).
- When CDA 2.0 was launched with its more advanced knowledge base and use of technology, there was external concern that a sizeable proportion of the 20,000 practitioners served annually would not be able to access the new CDA due to its online and computer-exam enhancements. Nevertheless, today almost all candidates complete computerized exams and most apply online.[23]
- Well before the deadline, Head Start staff met and exceeded federal goals that 50% of classrooms have a lead teacher with a bachelor's degree.[24]

RESPECTFUL BEHAVIOR

Rewarding the accomplishments of our workforce can be challenging for many reasons, not the least of which is the public policy and funding structures that influence how program days are organized and staffed. Balancing strategic priorities to highlight Respect for staff needs undoubtedly will stimulate field-wide creativity about how to tackle this unrelenting Goliath. Respectful behavior can release unrealized shared power.

What unites those who care about early childhood education—if there is any factor that feels universally "right"—is the robust understanding that our work has purpose. Without question, early childhood educators in all roles generally share a sense that what we do has value and meaning in the lives of children and families.[25] This is a uniquely powerful source of self- and field-wide Respect and motivation for change.

Practitioners, we believe, share the conclusion stated plainly in the 2015 Institute of Medicine and National Research Council report, *Transforming the Workforce for Children Birth to Age 8*:

Adults who are under-informed, underprepared, or subject to chronic stress themselves may contribute to children's experiences of adversity and stress and undermine their development and learning.[26]

PROFILE OF ROBERT GUNDLING, SENIOR CONSULTANT, BETTER FUTURES, LLC

To Robert Gundling, Respect in the early care and education field means meeting people where they are and recognizing they all have something to contribute—whether or not they have a college degree.

"We have to honor and Respect what our workforce faces in under-resourced communities," says Gundling. "Some experienced welfare reform to work; they are products of the discrimination of the public school system in this country."

Gundling has held multiple positions in the field, including being a kindergarten teacher, teaching college courses, working at the state policy level in Pennsylvania, leading centers, and serving as a professional development specialist for CDA candidates who observes CDA candidates as part of the Council's certification process. He now works as a consultant to early care and education programs and recently became president of the NAEYC affiliate in Washington, DC (DCAEYC).

He describes an experienced provider at a center in southeast DC who enrolled in an online associate's degree program but grew discouraged after encountering "a professor with an attitude." It was through encouragement and support from Gundling and her peers that she ultimately received her degree.

"We're seeing in the District that cohorts of teachers at centers and homes have a higher percentage of people completing a degree," he says. "That's not rocket science. The group forms a culture and it's supporting one another."

He wants the DCAEYC to be that source of support and engagement for teachers—at whatever level they can participate.

"We want them to be engaged, but we're not going to tell them what engagement means for them," he says. "We're going to have a boatload of educational opportunities for dialogue."

Gundling is also not afraid to talk about money. By 2020, he says, preschool teachers in the District will be required to have degrees and are even eligible for scholarships, but he understands how they get "demoralized and frustrated" when they don't see increases in pay.

"They get a degree and don't get an increase? What was the point?" he asks. "We have to decide what it costs. Who is going to pay the bill?"

Similarly, it is "through the quality work of these adults that the nation can make it right from the very beginning for all of its children."[27]

There are Goliathan expectations, burdens, and opportunities for the teaching workforce.

If the IOM report represents shared understandings—and we believe that it does—then we demonstrate "recognition" Respect by engaging practitioners in change processes. As a collaborative field, we should:

- employ considerations that are accessible to practitioners
- provide practitioners with genuine reasons for change
- act toward them only in ways to which they can give rational consent
- be willing to listen to them and take their feedback seriously
- promote autonomy and the conditions for it

In other words, respectful behavior requires a balance of actions that allow for the agency of practitioners.

Unfortunately, this balance is undermined, and a "Respect" dilemma for the field emerges when "professionalizing the field" puts a spotlight on changing the individual worker, rather than on changing the systems that create, suppress, and sustain lower educational attainment, wages, and regard for the professional who actually works with young children. A disproportionate focus on the weaknesses of the early childhood educator workforce, rather than acknowledging their contributions and predicaments, is a disrespectful deficit focus that is anathema to our field's strategic objectives to become a more cohesive voice for children and for ourselves.

THE TIME TO WAIT HAS PASSED!

In 1989, Whitebook, Howes, and Phillips released a National Child Care Staffing Study that put a spotlight on the low wages and high turnover of early childhood education staff, noting that these issues had a dire impact on children.

In 2000, the National Research Council wrote:

> The time is long overdue for society to recognize the significance of out-of-home relationships for young children, to esteem those who care for them when their parents are not available, and to compensate them adequately.[28]

In 2014, replicating their initial workforce study, Whitebook and her colleagues found conditions for staff largely unimproved. They wrote:

Another 25 years is too long to wait for improvements in early childhood jobs . . . our research and policy work has demonstrated how the status quo short-changes children, families, and the workforce itself. The time is long overdue for moving from the question of why we must improve early childhood jobs to a focus on how to make it happen.[29]

Now, at the end of 2017, the degree of change is not impressive. A *New York Times* editorial[30] put it this way:

The labels "low-skilled" or "unskilled" workers—the largest demographic being adult women and minorities—often inaccurately describe an individual's abilities, but play a powerful role in determining the opportunities to which they are exposed. The consequences are not only severe, but incredibly disempowering: poverty-level wages; erratic schedules; the absence of retirement planning, health benefits, paid sick or family leave; and the constant threat of being replaced.

Instead of improved job quality, the rewards for task-oriented workers are pats on the back and the constant encouragement to aspire for something better. Convincing these workers that their treatment is temporary, that if they just keep working harder, learn to do their tasks more quickly, more efficiently, and more fluidly, they will eventually surpass it—this is a myth we can't keep telling.

> I think it's too bad that our early educators are carrying this amazing responsibility yet they are for the most part working poor. It does a disservice to the workers, to the families, and to the children. I think people who should be excited about doing this work, and are excited about doing this work, are leaving because they cannot afford their lives. They are penalized for staying in the field because they cannot afford to support their own family.
>
> —Brenda Powers from Massachusetts

"They" aren't good enough? They are advancing the field en masse—in ways that only "they" can. We achieve balance when it is understood that "fixing" the early childhood educator will not resolve the asymmetrical power dynamics that surround the field of early childhood education. We achieve balance when we understand that a professional field is one that encourages respectful workplaces with productive and engaged employees committed to the next generation of world citizens.

Achieving Balance: What We Must Add as We Professionalize

In this chapter, we emphasize the importance of Respect as a Guiding Principle for advancing the field of early childhood education. Here are four areas of focus on Respect that we "must add" in efforts to professionalize the field.

1. As we work for change, we must add alignment among early childhood educators who work in different contexts. We no longer can merely "tolerate" parallel play among us.
2. As we work toward change, our largest focus must be on system building and "professional capital" rather than the capital or deficits of individuals. Fullan and Hargreaves[31] remind us that systems for building the teaching profession in the United States contrast sharply with strategies used in other countries.

   > We have directly studied, worked with, and worked in other successful countries, and they do not adopt the strategies of rewarding or punishing individual teachers with measures like test-driven, performance-based pay, or concentrate their energies on the extremes of competence with gushing teacher-of-the-year ceremonies or gung-ho proposals to remove the bottom 5 percent of educators from classrooms.[32]

   Observing the decline of the teaching profession in the United States, Fullan and Hargreaves found in international studies that successful countries develop the whole profession. They argue that human capital cannot be accumulated by focusing on individuals. Human capital must be complemented by social capital. "Without a strong and relentless focus on what we call 'professional capital,' U.S. policymakers will continue to miss lessons from other countries about how they produce teacher fulfillment and effectiveness, and to misread warning signs here at home as well."[33]
3. As we work toward change, we must take care that our messages acknowledge, appreciate, and Respect the contributions of the front-line workforce; emphasize strategies for practitioners' economic security; and improve staff working conditions. Indeed, the field cannot professionalize in an environment that does not honor staff. We must recognize that, without altering some of the fundamental aspects of work in the field—compensation, benefits, working conditions— increased qualifications and requirements are unlikely to advance the field but instead will become a pipeline to other occupations or to other sectors of education.
4. As we work toward change, we must act on workforce issues with urgency. We no longer can keep asking the workforce to wait patiently while attainment of a degree, achievement of program accreditation, rating by a quality rating improvement system (QRIS), and a myriad of other important strategies are pursued. The time for waiting has passed.

Facing Goliath: Affirmations

As the field moves toward greater professionalization, it is important that we acknowledge and demonstrate absolute dignity for practitioners and allies who work in any context for the field of early childhood education. We affirm:

We are worthy of Respect!

Our worth is inherent in who we are. We receive gratitude and appreciation for the work that we do with young children and their families. Our contributions are held in high esteem. We are encouraged by others, and we encourage ourselves. Everything is working together for our good. We are dynamic examples of love, peace, and service in the world.

Our contributions matter—a lot!

Our impact on the world is enormous. On a daily basis, we care for and educate more than 12 million children[34]—that's almost 70% of our nation's children under age 6.[35] We play a significant role in the lives of children and their families. The entire business and economic structure of our society relies upon our service, as well as our knowledge and skills.

We have a safe and productive work environment.

Just as children's environments support or impede their learning, our work environments promote or hinder our effectiveness. We have beautiful and supportive working conditions so we can do our best work in our workplaces. The words around us are helpful and positive. We want to be here!

We are economically secure.

Our needs are met and we are self-reliant. We have a stable income. All the resources we need are available to us now and in the foreseeable future. We are immersed in abundance. From this position of plenty, we are exceptionally generous toward others. We are grateful for what we have. This is our season for grace and favor!

Reflect on the Guiding Principle of *Respect*

When you practice gratefulness, there is a sense of respect toward others.

—Dalai Lama, spiritual leader of Tibet

1. As you reflect on Chapter 1, what are the main ideas about Respect that are meaningful to you in your work in the field of early childhood education?
2. In these Guiding Principles, we have described early childhood educators as people whose profession is *highly valued, of deferred value, and undervalued all at once!*
   Do you agree? Cite examples.
3. What do early childhood educators need in order to do their best work?
4. Cite an example of your experience of listening to multiple perspectives and multiple truths. Describe that experience. What was the impact of that experience on you?
5. What are the next steps that you and your colleagues can take to get more Respect?

CHAPTER 2

Competence

Staff working with young children historically have had a wide range of preparation experiences—some that entail formal education and some that do not. In a field where most programs for young children are considered to be mediocre at best,[1] most practitioners do not have college degrees. Yet, specialized training for staff is related to better outcomes for children, and the focus on increasing the field's collective Competence is critical and undeniable.

In recent years, the primary strategy to increase Competence has been to accelerate academic degree requirements for the early childhood education workforce. But let's look again: Is degree attainment a sufficient proxy for Competence for early childhood educators? And what is the pathway forward to define field-wide competencies?

WHAT IS COMPETENCE? WHAT ARE COMPETENCIES?

Competence—like Respect—is a Guiding Principle that is used widely but has many diffuse meanings and interpretations. To be Competent is to have the ability to do something successfully, proficiently, and/or efficiently—to have the knowledge, skills, attitudes, and experiences that enable a person to act effectively in a wide variety of situations. In addition, Competence can include relatively enduring characteristics of people, such as values and motive dispositions, that consistently distinguish outstanding from typical performance in a given job or role.

Competence is a performance criterion, while *competencies* are the observable and measurable behaviors driving the Competence. In other words, a person executes competencies to demonstrate that he or she is Competent.

WHY COMPETENCIES MATTER

For individuals, performance competencies—not job tasks—are what is needed to be successful in their work. For our profession, competencies:

- establish the field's professional identity and distinctive contribution by differentiating an early childhood educator from other professionals, such as nurses or social workers
- set the tone and context in which our work is carried out
- provide a structured guide that enables the field to define, develop, identify, and evaluate the scope of work or expected behaviors

Specific competencies matter because a field of practice will find it difficult to predictably produce and develop superior performers without first identifying what superior performance is. Without clear competencies, the field offers young children widely different early learning experiences and varying levels of preparation for success in school and beyond.

THE DILEMMA

And therein lies the dilemma: There is no accepted and nationally agreed-upon standard for what constitutes a high-quality program of study for early childhood education practitioners generally or for practitioners in various roles (such as assistant or lead teacher).[2] Moreover, there is no accepted and agreed-upon practice or expectation for the qualifications of early childhood educators. Workforce qualifications vary by state and range from less than a high school education to specialized 4-year academic degrees.[3]

The dilemma occurs, however, when "professionalizing the field" emphasizes the qualifications of staff (i.e., degree attainment) without a consensus definition of the actual staff behaviors or competencies required to care for and educate young children.

How can we reliably or systemically produce "Competent" practitioners without defining the "competencies"?

We raise this question because competencies matter—we are not suggesting that degrees do not matter. (As early as 2008 we wrote a position paper signed by eight institutions recommending a bachelor's degree.)[4] Professionalization requires competencies, many of which are likely to be acquired through degrees.

Both competencies and degrees are important—but they should be both aligned with and distinguished from each other. At best, degree mandates without competencies might be an important, partial step on the path toward becoming a strong profession. A clear relationship between the two will necessitate a great deal of additional hard work—work that must not be deferred now that degree attainment is gaining momentum.[5]

ABOUT THE CDA CREDENTIALS

Since 1975, The CDA has played a significant role across the spectrum of early childhood education settings in the United States, from employer-sponsored child care, to QRIS systems, to federal government-funded entities, such as Head Start and military child-care programs. The CDA has stood the test of time—more than 420,000 early childhood educators have earned the CDA credential, with approximately 20,000 new CDAs and 18,000 renewal CDAs awarded each year.

The CDA focus is on demonstrated competency through a combination of a national exam of knowledge, significant experience working with children, and observed behaviors. The CDA is portable across states and school districts nationwide.

There are six core features of the CDA:

1. The CDA encompasses multiple sources of evidence, such as 120 hours of professional education in early childhood development, 480 hours of work experience, a professional portfolio that demonstrates an understanding of the competencies, feedback from families, a work-setting observation that demonstrates effective practice, and content knowledge via the CDA exam.
2. The CDA credentialing assessment represents an organized process, *a coherent sequence of learning experiences* aligned with defined learning outcomes, and a comprehensive system of assessment that ensures candidates master defined learning outcomes and—most important—can demonstrate them in practice.
3. The CDA includes a direct *observation*, by a Council professional development specialist, of the candidate in the work setting as a lead teacher.
4. The CDA can be conducted in *any language* that supports the language required by a teacher's daily work setting.
5. The CDA values *family engagement* by encouraging family members to provide feedback on a CDA candidate's Strengths and areas for professional development.
6. The CDA credential is a *pathway* to learning best teaching practices for many early educators, such as a lead teacher who already holds an academic degree, but needs to gain hands-on practical skill and competency in early care and education; an assistant teacher with experience, but little formal education; a family child-care provider who must improve the quality of his/her setting to meet licensing requirements; or a high school student interested in pursuing a career in working with young children.

COMPETENCIES BY PROXY

Without answering the question of competencies, the field of early childhood education has appropriated, with great vigor, the idea of baccalaureate degree attainment as a strategic priority. This strategic priority is not without reason: While there is no single measure of quality, there is wide agreement that high-quality early childhood education programs share similar characteristics, including well-trained staff, low child to teacher ratios, intentional curricula, culturally sensitive and developmentally appropriate activities, and positive teacher/student relationships.[6] Positive child outcomes are directly linked to the quality of instruction among classroom teachers and the quality of the programs in which they participate.[7]

Will degrees professionalize the field by bringing greater predictability and uniformity to early childhood education practice?

The focus on degree attainment has not occurred without controversy. Historically, early childhood education is a field of practice that has relied extensively on informal apprenticeship with a heavy dose of missionary zeal. However, as governments and systems (such as QRIS) increasingly have mandated, encouraged, or funded degree acquisition, the idea has grown in acceptance. Competence is a process of continuous improvement, ideally accompanied by reflective supervision and support.

> I have heard people say that the rigor of ECE higher ed programs and curricula is subpar. I heard a top legislator say that the rigor is so low and that the quality of the individuals participating and graduating from them is so bad it doesn't warrant the [funding] investment.
>
> —Robyn Lightcamp from Ohio

ACCELERATING DEGREE ACQUISITION

While this proxy strategy has not yielded a field-wide definition of competencies, it *has* successfully resulted in increasing the numbers of early childhood educators who hold credentials and degrees. Following declines in the number of center-based teachers with a 4-year degree from the late 1980s to the early 2000s, by 2013[8] about 45% of educators working with children aged 3–5 in center-based settings held a bachelor's degree or higher, 17% held an associate's degree, and 13% had completed high school or less. Early childhood educators working with infants and toddlers have less education, with only 19% reporting a bachelor's degree or higher, 15% an associate's degree, and 30% a high school diploma or less.

But increasing degree attainment is a different phenomenon than pro-fessionalizing the field, to the extent that professionalization requires co-herent, well-organized, and coordinated expectations for early childhood education competencies. The lack of these competencies is one reason some authors now argue that, in its present state, early childhood education is not a "profession" at all.[9] Without these competencies, others openly ques-tion the field's ability to achieve the "promise of preschool," especially in terms of outcomes for children who speak English as a second language, children who have special needs, and children from low-income families.[10]

**PROFILE OF BROCKLIN QUALLS,
EARLY CHILDHOOD CONSULTANT, MARYLAND**

When Brocklin Qualls went to enroll his son in an early childhood program, he told someone at the center that his child has an individual family service plan—a plan that specifies the services needed by a child under 3 with special needs.

"What, is that a disease?" the person asked—a response that reinforced for Qualls the need for early educators, particularly those working in child-care centers, to have training in working with families of children with special needs.

"It is mission critical for our infant and toddler teachers to really understand early intervention," says Qualls, who served at the Council for Professional Recognition as manager of domestic and international partnerships. He also directed parent services for Child Care Aware and has worked in Head Start and Early Head Start. "In training for teachers, I say, 'Those developmental milestones are your framework.'"

While teachers in Head Start and Early Head Start have access to early intervention experts, and preschool teachers in the District of Columbia Public Schools are supported by the special education department, providers in child care usually don't have such resources. That's why Qualls would like to see training on special needs become a stronger part of teacher preparation.

Even teachers who earn a bachelor's degree and teaching credential, Qualls says, often lack the skills to work with special needs children and their families. He also advises early childhood educators who work with infants and toddlers to spend time learning about preschoolers, and for preschool educators to learn more about infants and toddlers, so they can better understand development across the birth-to-5 age range.

"I talk to teachers about this all the time," Qualls says. "We can't leave out any communities that we serve."

DEGREE ATTAINMENT:
AN INSUFFICIENT PROXY FOR COMPETENCIES

Proxies, such as degrees, are incapable of standing in for competencies because the coherence of the degrees themselves depends on the establishment of competencies. Isolated and compartmentalized strategies (such as degree attainment in our diverse institutions) may be useful but they are:

- wholly insufficient for dealing with the core, fundamental issues of our field, such as articulating what early educators should know and be able to do
- best viewed as an important but partial step toward building the profession

Questions about the wholesale adoption of teacher education programs for practitioners who work with young children involve at least three issues: the adaptive pressures now besieging higher education, the strength of teacher education programs, and the programs' reliance on a K–12 framework. Let us take a look at these three variables.

Adaptive Pressures of Higher Education

Ironically, the field of early childhood education is using a college degree strategy at a time when institutions of higher education are facing complex adaptive pressures. Although college degrees continue to be highly valued as symbols of success, key stakeholders are asking challenging questions about the extent to which college is:

- affordable or accessible[11]
- a valuable investment[12]
- responsive to the growing numbers of adult learners[13]
- creating "workforce-ready" employees[14]

Across many disciplines, it is becoming increasingly clear that more education does not necessarily lead to better outcomes for the college graduate. Simply holding a degree is not a guarantee of skills or knowledge needed in today's economy.[15]

And for the early childhood educator there are two even more fundamental questions:

- If the field lacks consensus about what an educator should know and be able to do,[16] then what exactly are teacher preparation programs supposed to teach? In our view, Whitebook and her colleagues, in a report entitled *By Default or By Design?* rightly conclude, "Too often, highly diverse higher education programs are assumed to produce equivalent results."[17]

- If a profession is defined partly by its competencies, how do we build a distinctive profession when many practitioners hold degrees in majors that are not specialized courses of study in early childhood education? Almost all—93%—of early childhood education staff and directors with a bachelor's degree do not possess a degree specifically in early childhood education. Twenty-nine percent have a degree in other education, 7% in psychology, and 3% in sociology.[18]

Teacher Education Program Quality

Many media sources have reported that all teachers in Finland have a master's degree and that they get extraordinary results from their students. There are significant differences in teacher preparation experiences in the United States and in Finland. Teachers in Finland hail from the top 10% of their graduating class and they matriculate in a coherent teacher education system that ensures they have a serious grasp on academic content and are well equipped to problem-solve around the individual learning needs of their students.[19]

In the United States, outside of the specialized subjects of science and math, hundreds of studies have not resolved the question of whether master's degrees produce more effective teachers.[20] For example, the National Council on Teacher Quality[21] found that in 90% of the studies, a teacher's advanced degree either had no impact or, in some cases, actually had negative effects on student achievement.[22]

Harsh narratives fill the commentaries on teacher education: Sixty-one percent of educators report that they were inadequately prepared for the classroom. The nation's 1,450 teacher's colleges are viewed as historically weak, doing a mediocre job at best,[23] and insufficiently accelerating the quality of the teacher workforce. A 2014 report from New America concluded that there is "little evidence of nationwide improvements in teacher development" and "little to no evidence of sustained effort to improve the caliber and training of the country's workforce from birth through third grade."[24]

> There is a billboard along the highway I see from time to time that promotes an alternative teaching degree (directed at the early childhood field). It states: You want to teach? Anyone can teach!—And then it directs you to a website for further information. I think that perspective is damaging to our field.
>
> —Belinda Rojas from Texas

These findings are disturbing because for early childhood educators, training matters for both program quality and child outcomes.[25] It is well documented that teacher quality is the most important in-school factor impacting student achievement.[26]

Some unanswered queries about early childhood higher education include:

- the relative value of a bachelor's degree versus an associate's degree or other type of credential or experience-based competencies
- the distinction between degree attainment and actual teacher behaviors and other variables that influence program quality and child outcomes[27]
- the types of preparation programs and field experiences that have a measurable impact on educator practices and child outcomes

Reliance on a K–12 Education Framework

NAEYC's 2015 survey found that early childhood educators themselves, while open to the idea of minimum educational requirements, are evenly split when asked if requirements should be set at a bachelor's degree for a lead teacher and an associate's degree for an assistant teacher. However, early childhood educators clearly understand the relationship between compensation and degree attainment in K–12 public education.

K–12 teachers typically enter employment with a bachelor's degree. Not surprisingly, public prekindergarten programs have more uniform, and typically higher, education requirements, differentiating these programs from the diversity of education requirements in most community-based programs.

In public schools, more degrees typically result in higher compensation. Consequently we note that 52% of the nation's 3.3 million public school teachers have a master's degree or better.[28]

> There is a fundamental misunderstanding about what the teacher's role is in early childhood because we have this idea that there is a teacher's role as it is understood in elementary education that can simply just be pushed down to younger children without changing the way we engage with those children.
>
> —Kay Lisseck from Massachusetts

Largely due to compensation issues, many early childhood educators seek public school employment once they earn a bachelor's degree. Not surprisingly, public school–sponsored centers pay the highest wages in the field.[29] And, compensation parity for early childhood education programs not in public schools typically is defined using K–12 education as a benchmark.[30]

Although a proven compensation strategy, the effectiveness of the bachelor's degree in preparing teachers for K–12 public education has been studied for decades and the result is not a resounding vote of confidence for either teacher preparation programs or child outcomes. Numerous studies show that many newly hired public school teachers are unqualified for the job.[31]

We observe, in public education, that accelerating degree requirements has not necessarily led to better outcomes for children, specifically for poor children of color.[32] Despite the high levels of academic preparation of public school teachers, only about one-third of children in the United States can read proficiently in 4th grade.[33]

> Are teacher preparation programs really representing what's needed to be an effective early education professional in the field?
>
> —Pamela Perrino from Ohio

Public schools have been offering support to preschool children for a long time, and this trend appears to be accelerating, particularly for 4-year-olds. Some school settings appear to be doing an excellent job of delivering developmentally appropriate practice.[34] Nevertheless, we ask: What are the shared and divergent professional development experiences and competencies that should be expected when young children are in public schools? What are the similarities and differences in expected competencies between early childhood and elementary education, if any?

- Careful attention must be given to issues such as the program philosophy, assessment practices, curriculum, physical learning environment, learning materials, and parent and community engagement, to name a few.
- Typically, funding strategies are a major source of difference between public schools and early childhood education programs. K–12 education receives about 10% of its funding from the federal government, which is the reverse of early childhood education, which receives about 90% of its funding from the federal government.[35]

In our view, at the current time, a well-educated workforce, including but not limited to educators who have completed bachelor's degrees, is useful for many reasons, but it is not a sufficient proxy for the field-wide delineation of competencies. We agree with the IOM report, which states:

> Given that empirical evidence about the effects of a bachelor's degree is inconclusive, a decision to maintain the status quo and a decision to transition to a higher level of education as a minimum requirement entail similar uncertainty and as great a potential consequence for outcomes for children. The

committee therefore makes the recommendation to transition to a minimum expectation of a bachelor's degree for lead educators working with young children.[36]

We interpret the IOM findings to mean that change is not optional. And the need for change is even more pronounced because few states have qualification requirements in line with the IOM recommendations: Ten states have no educational requirements for center-based lead teachers, and an additional 23 states have no requirements for regulated home-based providers.

Only 11 states set a minimum requirement, for some early childhood educators working outside the public pre-K system, that includes demonstration of foundational knowledge by earning a national Child Development Associate Credential™ or participation in vocational education; only Georgia and Vermont require this for both center- and home-based providers. Of the 44 states (including the District of Columbia) with public pre-K programs, only 23 require a minimum of a bachelor's degree for all lead pre-K teachers.[37]

BEYOND DEGREES: MOVING TOWARD COMPETENCIES

We cannot change what we do not face. To develop competencies in a way that will truly professionalize the field, at least four elements are required: shared understanding among key stakeholders, credible teaching leadership, content that is translated into observable performance by practitioners, and career progression.

Shared Understanding Among Key Stakeholders

Because competencies are context-dependent, there is no universal or absolute definition of the knowledge or skill that defines a competency. This is why field-wide collaboration among key stakeholders is essential to any effort to define competencies.

A savvy, trustworthy community of practice must come together to consider the positions and requirements of all relevant and diverse constituents. This collaborative effort must be established as an autonomous forum. It must be perceived as having a collective level of expertise sufficient to create, define, and distribute knowledge regarding the critical issues about which the field is passionate. Such a group would be a driver of the field's advancement and must include the perspectives of front-line staff.

One of the first challenges of this leadership group would be to establish clarity about the field's defining purpose. The field initially must do the hard work of determining the primary and secondary motives for the field's work; the extent to which program setting, the ages of children served, or auspices inform the field's purpose; the target of benefits of the field's work; and how issues of race, language, or social class inform its purpose.[38]

This type of field-wide collaboration is certain to be challenging due to the competition among the many different voices and organizations that will want to be heard. Yet, the professionalization of the field cannot proceed without it.

Credible Teaching Leadership

As we work for change, competencies must be conveyed by diverse and experienced faculty and trainers who possess both practical field experience as well as deep understanding of the field's formulations and theory. This goal is impacted by at least two variables: the proliferation of training options in our field and questions about the faculty themselves.

Today, many college faculty are described as having a lack of training, experience, and expertise in early childhood education settings; a lack of diversity; and insufficient preparation to meet the needs of their adult students/practitioners who are "nontraditional students."[39]

Additionally, there are a growing number, variety, and complexity of online and in-person early childhood education training sites, independent trainers, and other preparation programs that compete with traditional higher education programs. The proliferation of community-based training through resource and referral agencies, employers, and a wide variety of private enterprises results in uneven quality and covers a wide range of content areas. Field-wide competencies are needed now more than ever to help bring coherent expectations to the work of training institutions.

Creating criteria to identify the professional development experiences that will provide both comprehensive training and solid practical experience in a range of early learning programs is a field-wide responsibility.

Performance

The Council of Regional Accrediting Commissions reminds us that "while competencies can include knowledge or understanding, they primarily emphasize what students can do with their knowledge . . . because competencies are often anchored to external expectations, such as those of employers."[40]

Despite the upswing in degree attainment, especially for preschool centers, "the word on the street" often expresses uncertainty about the practical utility of the degrees in terms of actually working with real children in the field's various settings, such as center-based or family child care. Here are two typical reflections about the relationship between degrees and performance:

- Commenting on his large staff, Louis Finney, executive vice president of children and Head Start services in Florida, observed that, often, Classroom Assessment Scoring Systems™ (CLASS) scores—a measure of actual interactions with children—for his CDA and bachelor's degree teachers are similar—and that the scores in centers and family child care are also similar.
- It is not uncommon for a recent college graduate to encounter difficulty translating abstract theories about learning and development into actual classroom practices that promote specific outcomes. A young professional who wishes to remain anonymous told us: "I have a bachelor's degree and I know that's why I was hired as the lead teacher. But when I went to the program there were two older women with CDAs. They had to teach me everything. I felt bad because I knew I made more money than they did, and I recognized that they had better skills."

Valora Washington hears these comments often in her role as CEO of the Council for Professional Recognition. Because the CDA requirements combine work experience with training and assessment of actual performance, it is not uncommon for many employers to comment favorably on the CDA's utility as a tool for workforce readiness. This is also true because the CDA is portable across states and has served as the field's premier credential for more than 40 years. Employers and CDA candidates know more about what can be expected in the CDA learning process than they know about the curriculum of any given university or training program.

> Those who are practicing in the field, in the classroom, know the value of that hands-on experience and really live the theory. How well are we incorporating that value in our higher ed coursework and programs?
>
> —Maureen Boggs from Ohio

Nevertheless, the CDA is "the best first step" in a professional journey that, like academic degrees, exists in an extremely diverse public policy framework. Since 2009, NAEYC has offered Standards for Initial and Advanced Early Childhood Professional Preparation Programs. Currently, however, less than one-fourth of all eligible programs have earned either the initial or the advanced certification. In addition, states vary in the extent to which they have either developed competencies or had them incorporated into their institutions of higher education.

In their review of 2- and 4-year institutions, researchers from the University of North Carolina found that some programs addressed working with children across the birth-to-8 age range, while others focused more specifically on preschoolers and children in the early grades. Across 19 different topic areas related to the early childhood profession, the researchers identified some significant gaps. For example, "about 20 percent of CDA and associate's programs and about 10 percent of bachelor's and master's programs did not require any coursework in working with bilingual children learning English as a second language."[41]

The North Carolina researchers also looked at practicum requirements for early educators and found that some programs—specifically 4% of associate's and bachelor's degree programs and 33% of master's programs—required no student teaching or field placement experience. Of all

---

PROFILE OF LOUIS FINNEY,
EXECUTIVE VICE PRESIDENT OF CHILDREN AND HEAD START SERVICES,
LUTHERAN SERVICES FLORIDA

Overseeing more than 1,000 Head Start teachers for one of the largest early learning organizations in the country, Louis Finney has a strong understanding of what it takes for teachers to be successful in working with young children.

While he has at times hired graduates right out of college for teaching positions, Finney says that if the degree program doesn't offer at least 1 year of early childhood practicum experience, teachers are less likely to be successful.

That's why Finney looks for teachers with both a degree *and* a CDA credential—a combination that gives teachers both the knowledge and the practical experience they need to be prepared for a variety of classroom situations.

"I've had side by side a CDA and a degreed teacher, and some of those CDA teachers were just as good and sometimes better," Finney says. "They are still able to articulate and manage that classroom as well."

Finney adds that a degree on its own shouldn't qualify someone to be a teacher. Training specifically in early childhood education, covering areas such as brain development, teaching strategies, and how to work with children who have special needs, should be the requirement. A CDA, on the other hand, gives early educators the experience they need to determine whether they want a career in the field. "You've got to like working with young children everyday," he says.

In addition to his role at Lutheran Services Florida, Finney is vice president of the National Family Childcare Association, the founding president of the Greater Tampa Bay Area Chapter of the National Black Child Development Institute, and president of the Florida Head Start Association. A former Head Start student and an Army veteran, Finney brings a unique perspective to the early childhood field.

He wants the perception of early educators to change and knows that requiring teachers to have a degree is part of the process of professionalizing the field.

"We've got to remove ourselves from just caring for children," says Finney. "We are educating children."

the associate's degree programs, only 62% required practicum experience in working with infants and toddlers. In addition, students in only 41% of those 2-year programs gained experience working with children with disabilities. The researchers questioned whether teachers were gaining the depth necessary to be highly qualified to teach children at each age covered. In other words, there is a training gap between the college classrooms and practitioners actually planning a day of activities for children.[42]

Studies by Boyd-Swan and Herbst found a consistent theme of decreasing returns to teacher qualifications by employers: Center-based employers may not hire the most qualified applicants; job seekers with a bachelor's degree are no more likely to receive an interview than their counterparts at the associate's degree level; and those job applicants with more early childhood education experience are less likely to receive an interview than those with less experience.[43]

To earn credibility, early childhood teacher education must use "authentic assessment"—that is, it must help students transfer skills from learning experience to real-world application. Such levels of authenticity in assessment are generally possible only through the real-life execution of competencies or through high-fidelity role plays and simulations, all of which are very expensive, time consuming, and labor intensive to create.

CDA PROFESSIONAL DEVELOPMENT SPECIALIST SYSTEM

In addition to successfully passing a national exam that tests the candidate's knowledge, and completing 480 hours of experience working with children, every CDA candidate is observed by one of the 8,000 Professional Development Specialists™ (PDS) in the Council for Professional Recognition's national network. A PDS is an early childhood professional who is trained, contracted, and endorsed by the Council to utilize his or her expertise to facilitate the final stages of the credentialing process for candidates within local communities.

During the CDA Verification Visit™, PDS observers use the Review. Observe. Reflect. (R.O.R.) Model™ to facilitate the CDA assessment of a candidate based on the candidate's self-reflection and professional growth. The PDS is expected to deliver professional development experiences to candidates by incorporating coaching skills, early childhood education expertise, and cultural sensitivity. The evidence collected by the PDS is designed to distinguish competent candidates from those who are in need of more training. This is based on candidates meeting the competency criteria established by the CDA Competency Standards.

CAREER PROGRESSION

A key task for the professionalization of the field will be the creation of sturdy and understandable field-wide career ladders, pathways, and lattices.[44] These terms are used as metaphors to describe how early childhood educators can progress within our profession from entry-level positions to higher levels of pay, skill, responsibility, or authority. Career progress can be vertical (a ladder of upward mobility within an occupational field) or lateral (a pathway that broadens skills or builds bridges). Career pathways can have tracks (that is, practitioners can deepen their knowledge as a teacher and would not have to become a director to have increased professional recognition). Career pathways also consist of networks that can help practitioners who want to experiment in a related field (such as a move from teaching to home visiting).

Because many practitioners are working adults, career mapping is a valuable tool to help them think strategically about how to grow professionally. For example, how will the field capture skills learned on the job, give credit for prior learning, or create new learning while guiding students to discard practices that are no longer effective? Several policy frameworks are promoting and supporting answers to these questions and the development of career pathways, including the IOM and NRC study, the Workforce Innovation and Opportunities Act, and the Child Care Development Block Grant Act of 2014.

As the policy landscape shifts, countless program directors face the dilemma of "what to do with Miss Lucy," a prototypical long-term employee

---

We have been able to lobby successfully for significant changes to the QRIS process in Oregon, which now recognizes on many levels—in addition to degrees—the skills, competencies, languages, and cultural diversity of our staff as indicators of high quality. As a result, all of our programs are now rated 5 stars and the QRIS standards and Head Start performance standards are in alignment.

Institutions of higher education could add to the conversation about competencies and training, but they won't step up to the plate. Their programs are generally not taught by people with practical experiences in the field, so they can't offer the full picture—just the theory. When you think about it, would you feel comfortable stepping on a plane if it was piloted by people who were trained like institutions of higher education train our teachers?

—Ron Herndon from Oregon

with strong relationships with children and families but who does not hold, and perhaps has no intention of acquiring, a formal degree. The program's eligibility for funding and for meeting quality rating requirements may be enhanced by the presence of the degree holder, but losing "Miss Lucy" might have a qualitatively negative effect on the actual program.

The field itself offers little structured guidance in addressing these challenges—other than to give preference to the degree holder. "Miss Lucy" may be reclassified as an assistant teacher—but her actual role and expected competencies remain undefined.

Field-wide career pathways[45] would support these decisions through the following (among other goals):

> establishing clearly defined roles (such as teacher assistant, lead teacher, assistant director, director) and common terminology across settings and sectors; setting qualification targets for degrees for early childhood educators, with reasonable timeframes to meet requirements; establishing an agreed-upon sequence of the credentials that reflects increasing levels of knowledge and competence, grounded in the science of child development and in effective, developmentally appropriate teaching practices and program leadership; [and] creating clarity about different career choices and how to achieve them, regardless of the point at which the individual enters the pathway.[46]

Pathways, and career progression, often are viewed as the acquisition of increasing numbers of degrees, credentials, and certifications. Some educators express cautions about this: Paul Thomas describes himself as "one of those people in education with a string of education degrees—undergraduate and two graduate degrees in education." The real challenge of teacher quality, Thomas contends, is to build a teaching profession that is a "challenging discipline" that moves teachers along a pathway to becoming both "master teachers" and "autonomous scholars." Reflecting on teacher licensing and certification, Thomas remarks:

> The political and public discourse about teacher education has been historically condescending and recently further eroded by the essential failure of teacher education: the technocratic and bureaucratic nature of certification. . . . We must acknowledge that think-tank advocacy and reports are often agenda-driven and not well suited for education reform.[47]

Achieving Balance: What We Must Add as We Professionalize

In this chapter, we emphasize the importance of Competence and competencies as Guiding Principles for advancing the field of early childhood education, and give considerable attention to the role of higher education institutions, since degree attainment often is used as a proxy for Competence. Here are four areas of focus on Competence that we "must add" to efforts to professionalize the field.

1. As we consider the creation of competencies, we must add our own *creativity and expertise*; let's not merely copy, adopt, or mimic what other fields are doing, whether it is K–12 education, nursing, or other professions. Let's learn from others and realize that adaptive leadership is required as we build consensus around competencies for early childhood education.

2. A second must-add is appropriate financing for the field of early childhood education. Public funds are needed to both enable practitioners to better support themselves[48] and earn the degrees now being promulgated. The field continues to experience a lack of pay parity for the degrees already earned. This amounts to an inequity that must be resolved. The funding issue represents a substantial asymmetrical conflict for the field—a conflict that is beginning to be perceived as an achievable policy goal.[49]

> It's been a challenge to hire teachers who have their bachelor's. A lot of people who get their bachelor's want higher pay for teaching.
>
> —Cindy Rojas Rodriquez from Texas

3. A third must-add is the policy work that must be done to recalibrate the current low levels of entry qualifications for early childhood education staff, with mandatory *competencies*, once they are established. Action will be needed to facilitate states' alignment with the field's own definition of staff qualifications.

4. And the fourth must-add is deliberate attention to questions about *Equity*. To what extent, and in which ways, are teacher education programs transmitters of asymmetrical conflict and power? A team of researchers found that teacher education focuses more on "difference" and less on Equity, shared power, and redistribution of resources. As a result, teachers may develop a framework for thinking of children from a variety of populations as "disadvantaged," "deficient," and "deviant" or "at risk."[50]

> Why should anyone spend $20,000 to get a BA when the profession won't pay them a living wage?
>
> —Ron Herndon from Oregon

Indeed, teacher education programs are social institutions that reflect historical, political, and social arrangements that generally benefit groups with power and privilege; and determine which "voices" will be heard or silenced, and ultimately how social power and advantage will be distributed in society.

Facing Goliath: Affirmations

As the field moves toward greater professionalization, it is important that we define the observable and measurable behaviors or characteristics that articulate its distinctive contributions. We affirm:

We are growing in knowledge, experience, and expertise.

We give 100% to our efforts. We ask for advice and seek insights from others. We release all criticism. We are motivated and dedicated. We are talented and our minds are open. We set goals and acknowledge our achievements. We are now making amazing progress toward all of our goals.

We teach others as we learn.

We are always learning and demonstrating what we know. We share what we learn with others. We are all learners, doers, and teachers. Whatever we conceive and believe, we can achieve. We learn and teach with open enthusiasm and passion. And we share our passion with others.

We are able and highly competent.

We reflect on our situations. We remain confident of our ability to succeed. We are creative and responsive to the individual needs of the people we serve. Every day in every way, we are becoming better and better. What we imagine we can do, we can do. We receive wisdom and knowledge every moment of our lives. We are completely adequate for the demands of any situation.

We always do our best!

Being our best is not just what we do. It is a state of mind that drives all of our actions and behaviors. We are wise, efficient, courageous, and strong leaders. Excellence is our standard of service. We work with joy and confidence.

Reflect on the Guiding Principle of *Competence*

If you think you can do it, that's confidence. If you do it, that's competent.

—Original source unknown (quoted by Morris Baxter, author of *The Morris Code*)

1. How would you rate your confidence on a scale of 1 to 10, with 10 being the highest?
2. How would you rate your Competence on a scale of 1 to 10, with 10 being the highest?
3. Name the next three steps that you think should be taken to professionalize the early childhood education field.
4. Among our decisions as a field we will need to establish minimum preparation qualifications for various roles. What do you think? Please complete the following grid. Compare your responses with those of your colleagues and with local requirements.

ROLE	High school diploma	CDA	Associate's degree	Bachelor's degree	Master's degree
Lead teacher					
Assistant teacher					
Supervisor or director of a program					
Coach					
College faculty					
Trainer or faculty member					
Select another role					

CHAPTER 3

Strengths

The clarion call to professionalize the field is a response to factors that are wrong with the profession and the Competence of the people who work in it. Here we would like to draw attention to factors about early childhood education that are assets—which we want to preserve—as we strengthen our professional culture.

THE ADAPTIVE CHALLENGE:
WHAT'S WORTH KEEPING?

As the adaptive leadership theorists Ron Heifetz and Marty Linsky[1] point out, being an architect of change is just as much about deciding what is essential and what needs to be brought forward as it is about what needs to be left behind. These decision points require us to face really difficult choices between competing values. This can be painful work—and that's what makes leadership so challenging.

Are there only two choices: Miss Lucy or the newly minted bachelor's-prepared teacher? Will the profession's change strategies leave someone or something important behind? Are there gaps between our values and professionalization process? What else might we do to face our adaptive challenges?

To answer these types of questions, Heifetz's practical recommendation is that we "get on the balcony" in order to see key patterns. View these patterns through the eyes of the practitioners. Then ask: "What is worth preserving as we change?"

When describing adaptive leadership, Marty Linsky gives an analogy[2]: Plants and animals evolve; while they give up part of their DNA as a species, they preserve most of it. Our DNA as human beings is 96 to 97% the same as chimpanzees' DNA—a huge percentage that is the same and a very small percentage that is different. Yet, we are incredibly distinct from chimpanzees. In this analogy, 3% makes the difference between an ape and a person!

THE 3RD ALTERNATIVE

Stephen Covey, author of *The 7 Habits of Highly Effective People*,[3] developed a process of conflict resolution that he calls the 3rd Alternative,[4] which is the subject of his book of the same name. In it, he takes a more detailed look at habit six: "synergize." Covey explains that, when engaged in a negotiation or confronted with a problem, most people aren't aware that a 3rd Alternative even exists.

The 3rd Alternative is distinct from compromise. According to Covey, 3rd Alternative thinking involves applying four *paradigms*: "I See Myself" (coming to know yourself), "I See You" (seeing others with the same respectfulness as you now see yourself), "I Seek You Out" (understanding others and their views), and "I Synergize with You" (a four-step process of arriving at synergy—"Ask the 3rd Alternative Question," "Define Criteria of Success," "Create 3rd Alternatives," and "Arrive at Synergy").

COMPETENCE AND IMPROVISATIONAL PERFORMANCE ART

In Chapter 2 on Competence, we emphasized the practitioners' skillful execution of a more well-defined scope of work targeted to achieve specific results, such as enhancing a child's vocabulary, mathematical reasoning, critical thinking, and other indicators of "school readiness." Typically, professionals think of these competencies as "hard skills."

But particularly when technical skills are equal, what makes one educator stand out over another? Are there dynamics of our profession that are the "DNA" of who we are? Is there a 3% of the early childhood education profession that makes all of the difference for children, families, and practitioners?

We affirm that skillful child caring and educating for "readiness" matter! Yet, we suspect that there are "softer skills" at the core of Competence—the symbolic 3%—that are part of the essence of the early childhood education profession. (The value of "soft skills" for early childhood educators may indeed be much greater than 3%!)

If we examine these soft skills, we will discover patterns that constitute the core DNA that must be preserved. Within these patterns, we find a professional culture that is deserving of our attention. Because after all, with humility, we recognize that teaching is not just a technical science. Teaching young children is also an improvisational performance art![5]

MAKING OUR CULTURE VISIBLE

Just as a fish may not be aware of water and the cloud has no concept of the sky, it may be difficult for us to see and fully appreciate the Strengths of our profession. Our field's culture is intangible—but it may be more definable when we look at it from the balcony.

How do we sense the presence of the 3%? Remember when you became a member of the field and you had that ethereal feeling that this was the right calling for you? Or when you are attending a conference and you "know" that there is a shared sense of the importance of our work and "ways of being"?

We acquire a professional culture in many ways. A field's culture takes hold through extensive personal contact and interaction, professional networks, and the trust we earn when we are with our colleagues. It's in the air—and we absorb it: the norms, assumptions, and customs of our field. There are patterns of collective behaviors, ways of interacting with one another, and approaches to the world that matter to "us" in "our culture."

Much of the culture of early childhood education is hidden from us in a myriad of unwritten rules or assumptions, which often are taken for granted, about "the way we are." But making our culture visible is part of what is required if we are to preserve it. To capture our 3%, we must prioritize our professional culture as an essential feature of occupational change.

And, just knowing that our culture is important is not sufficient to ensure that we will keep the qualities that matter. Indeed, the field may be at a disadvantage for creating a field-wide focus on cultural preservation because our professional focus has been more on "hard skills" and less on strategies that build a profession.

> When you begin to understand the gravity or immense responsibility that goes along with teaching young children, you begin to develop this moral drive that wants you to do the best you can for the children. We have an obligation to the children and families we serve. They deserve the best.
>
> —Cindy Rojas Rodriquez
> from Texas

Making our culture visible must encompass a shared vision that is just as important as developing other aspects of occupational Competence. Otherwise the field risks stimulating change that consists of mandates without meaning, a field with weakened roots.

"INTANGIBLES" DRIVE PERFORMANCE

Not convinced that soft skills matter? In a business context, Low, Kalafut, and Cohen describe soft skills as "intangibles" that drive performance.[6]

Intangibles, they state, are important because they create and cultivate a set of emotions (like loyalty to a brand). These authors advise us that the key sources of value creation have shifted from the tangible to the intangible, and that they have frequent and usually positive spillover effects. Human capital is a top driver of intangible value; after all, the field of early childhood *education* is only as good as the early childhood *educators*.

For early childhood educators, we categorize our intangibles—the 3%—in two categories.

- *Personal Character Qualities* that practitioners elicit and inspire in others such as:
  - » love
  - » commitment with pride and enthusiasm about the work that we perform
  - » trust
- *Relationships* with children and families that enable early childhood educators—perhaps more than other education professionals—to:
  - » engage passionately with children and families
  - » literally "speak their language"
  - » accept and appreciate diversity
  - » offer service flexibility

Let us take a look at these factors as ideals and also consider potential cautions that could undermine these intangibles as we professionalize the field of early childhood education.

Personal Character Qualities

Occupational love, commitment, and trust are key factors to consider as we address the early childhood educators' Competence—the 3% difference.

What's Love Got to Do with It? In life as well as in a career, love may not be enough, but it is certainly *essential*! There is ample evidence that early childhood educators love their work.[7] Researcher Laura Colker found that most people enter our field with altruistic motivations and a sense of destiny; we want to make a mark, a difference in the world.[8] In

What is needed for quality early care and education? Staff who are compassionate, committed, and love the work and believe in the potential of their children, families, and communities. Staff who understand and respect the communities and cultures their children come from. Staff who understand the challenges in the communities and how families are impacted or affected by them. Staff who are willing to get involved— to go the extra step and seek out resources and services that can help lift people up.

—Ron Herndon from Oregon

PROFILE OF CECILE TOUSIGNANT, CHILD TOOLS CONSULTING

As an early childhood coach and trainer in Massachusetts, Cecile Tousignant says it's the relationships that early childhood educators form with children and their families that can be their greatest Strength.

Additional requirements and regulations being placed on teachers, however, sometimes can stand in the way of forming those bonds, she says. Using hand-washing as one example, Tousignant suggests that having children always practice counting to 10 while they're washing their hands "can distract from the teacher's interaction with children."

Using classroom transition times to boost children's academic skills is a recommended strategy, but when teachers have strong relationships with children, they know which children might need extra help moving to the next activity or getting ready to go outside.

"Children are not going to learn from a teacher with a bachelor's or a CDA or any training whatsoever unless those children have a relationship with that teacher," says Tousignant, who transformed a nightclub into a child-care center in the mid-1970s and now provides coaching as part of the Massachusetts Department of Early Education and Care's Educator and Provider Support grant program.

When she visits Head Start classrooms or family child-care homes, Tousignant forms her own relationships with providers and "clears the air" before she focuses on areas where they need improvement in order to earn accreditation or a higher rating in the state's quality rating and improvement system. "I try to find out what their needs are," she says.

She also worries about the number of transitions young children, especially infants and toddlers, go through when their parents can't find or afford high-quality care. "It's so costly for families that they have to move the kid in between grandmother, uncle, and aunt," she says. "That's not best practice for children."

NAEYC's 2015 survey of early childhood educators,[9] those reporting said that the opportunity to work with children and help them succeed was what attracted them to the field. Ninety-one percent indicated, "I have always loved working with children." Nearly all early childhood educators believe that to be an "excellent" member of their profession, one must be passionate, patient, caring, and loving.

And the public also values this "soft" competency: Ninety-three percent of voters in the NAEYC survey indicated "patient and passionate teachers" as the number 1 component for ensuring quality in an early childhood education program. Over 80% of survey respondents said that early childhood

Sometimes we hear from programs talking about how difficult it is to find qualified personnel. They will also describe individuals who apply who really want to work in the field and have a passion for it, but yet they aren't encouraged or considered because of a perceived language barrier such as a thick accent. I think we are leaving a lot of potential staff resources on the table because of a tendency to look at individuals from a deficit perspective. There's an untapped workforce. We need to figure out how to recognize and utilize their potential. Instead of being seen as a potential strong asset whose language could enhance a program, they aren't even allowed to come to the table.

—Belinda Rojas from Texas

educators "genuinely care for the children they teach," "are compassionate," and "put children's interests before their own."

These intangibles clearly impact practitioner performance. A study in the *Harvard Business Review*[10] found that employees who feel love perform better. Similarly, Brady Wilson[11] explains that since "passion drives performance," leaders must understand that engaging people's hearts trumps engaging their minds. Wilson states that leaders who love believe in their people, pull out their highest good, serve their success, and challenge them.

Commitment: Ready to Grow and Change. In the NAEYC survey, the vast majority of educators see early childhood education as a rewarding career and as an opportunity to lay the foundation for children's school success. They say they want to make early childhood education their career for the foreseeable future. Educators are very open to the concept of increased occupational requirements in order to receive higher pay and benefits.

> It starts with having the patience, love, and desire to work in this field. How do we instill in a teacher the love of the field and the passion and compassion to take children and love them wherever they come from and wherever they are?
>
> —Cindy Rojas Rodriquez from Texas

Early childhood educators respond very positively to messages emphasizing their positions as role models in the lives of children and their ability to make a difference on behalf of long-term goals for those children. They experience daily "magic moments" with children.

Commitment is an essential Strength of the workforce, which intentionally must be nurtured and celebrated with the same vigor that degree acquisition is encouraged. In the K–12 context, teacher commitment has been found to be a critical predictor of teachers' work performance, absenteeism, burnout, and turnover, as well as an important influence on students' achievement and attitudes toward school.[12]

What does commitment look like? The new early childhood professional committed to this profession exhibits the following qualities:

- Is dedicated to children's learning and development, believing that all children can learn
- Feels rewarded by students' growth and successes (those "magic moments")
- Strongly identifies with the goals of the profession and desires to remain a part of it
- Sees commitment as part of his or her professional identity
- Belongs to early childhood education associations and develops a professional learning network
- Is a lifelong learner who engages in formal or informal continuous professional development

Although this idea of commitment may seem "patent" or "obvious," the issue is a matter for serious inquiry. The nature, life cycle, facilitators, and deterrents of commitment for early childhood educators is a topic that deserves a great deal more research and exploration.

In the context of practitioner Competence and compensation, how altruistic or self-sacrificing is this profession? How altruistic or self-sacrificing should it be? A balance between self-abnegation and self-interest is needed[13]—a complex balance that involves factors such as working conditions that are outside of the practitioner's influence. Clearly, teacher turn-

> Passion is important. I understand and agree that education is a big part of what makes a teacher, but if they don't have passion for what they are doing there's a problem. I have a teacher who does not have a college degree and she is an excellent teacher, and her passion is part of what makes her a great teacher.
>
> —Daniela Santos from Massachusetts

over does not rest solely with a lack of commitment. Chris Higgins states that, "in order to cultivate selfhood in students, teachers must bring to the table their own achieved self-cultivation, their commitment to ongoing growth, and their various practices, styles, and tricks for combating the many forces that deaden the self and distract us from our task of becoming."[14] In the words of Jean-Paul Sartre, "Commitment is an act, not a word."

Trust. NAEYC found that survey respondents also express high levels of trust in early childhood educators and child development experts. Practitioner performance is certainly likely to be enhanced by the intangible value of trust. Indeed, Stephen R. Covey[15] stated that the only sustainable competitive advantage that will long endure is the core competency of a high-trust culture. We note that he calls trust—an intangible, a soft skill—a "core competency."

His son, Stephen M. R. Covey, has written an informative and inspiring book, *The Speed of Trust*.[16] This book suggests that change strategies without trust pay high "taxes" in the form of redundancy, bureaucracy, politics, disengagement, turnover, customer churn, and fraud. Conversely, high trust creates "dividends," including stakeholder value, stronger partnering, heightened loyalty, improved collaboration, accelerated growth, and enhanced innovation. Also important in Covey's description of trust is the notion that it takes *both* character *and* Competence to build, sustain, or regain trust. That's why we encourage professional change processes to concentrate as much attention to the intangibles as to the competencies.

Relationships

We believe that an important reason for the high levels of trust given to early childhood educators is the strong relationships that practitioners develop with families. Families entrust their precious children to the hands of these practitioners every day, and many children actually spend more of their waking hours with the practitioners than with their families.

The relationships established by practitioners with families result from many factors. These factors include the cultural and language connections and the intimacy created by the nature of the interactions, as well as the field's historic focus on family choice and parent power.

Cultural Connections. Relationships are enhanced, we believe, by the diversity of the early childhood education workforce. Compared to all public school teachers, early childhood educators are more representative of community cultures, languages, and ethnicities.[17]

The field's focus on diversity is a professional asset developed over decades. Since the 1920s, "emphasis has been on the young child in the family and community."[18] Further, NAEYC has been a leader, "a genuine pioneer in the cultural diversity, multiculturalism, antibias movement."[19] Moreover, NAEYC standards and position statements continually have recognized that development and learning occur in a cultural context, and they have stressed the importance of reciprocal relationships with families. Taken together, the profession's focus reflects a deeply rooted Respect for diversity in the principles, practice, values, and science of early childhood education.[20]

Shared Language. Early childhood educators are more likely than other education professionals to literally "speak the same language" as families.

I feel it's really critical to be a part of the community as a school leader, and I know oftentimes it's hard to create boundaries professionally. I think that breaking down those barriers, by not seeing yourself as just being here at the school but allowing yourself to go out into the community and be part of the community, is so important, especially nowadays with all the stresses that people experience.

I had a student that was having behavior problems. He had just moved here from a neighboring community and he was really struggling behaviorally and having difficulty creating relationships with other peers. So, I visited his home and I was able to sit down with his mother and talk about what her hopes and dreams were for him. I saw the change in the child's reaction to me. I'd visited about four times by the end of the year. Through those visits, I also noticed a lot of Strengths her son had that were not necessarily perceived at school. I also found out that the mother was illiterate, which nobody knew beforehand. So, I was able to sit down with her and go through papers and guide her. She had always had a negative experience with education, and I was able to change that for her.

In future months as the mom learned to trust me, she turned to, rather than turned away from, the school. Her son is no longer at the school, but she still calls me when he's struggling and will talk to me about what's going on in her life. When there were problems, she came to me and asked for my help. That meant a lot to me.

—Christine Pruitt from Massachusetts

Staff with a first language other than English are the fastest growing segment of the workforce. In addition, they often have limited English proficiency (about 54% have this status).[21]

Growth in the linguistic diversity of the early childhood education workforce mirrors the population of the children served. Since 2000, 57% of the total population growth in the United States has taken place among immigrants and their children, and nearly 30% of all young children under 6 have at least one parent who speaks a language other than English. For these families with young children, the option of working with a same-language practitioner creates a cultural connection that is highly prized.[22]

Intimate Encounters. The relative intimacy of many early childhood education settings promotes relationships with families. For example, before their third birthday, many children are cared for in family child-care settings since many parents prefer to have their children supported in a home-like environment. For working families, family child care offers greater flexibility around atypical work schedules, compared with centers or schools. These factors stimulate interpersonal affection and connection.

Family Choice. Early childhood education programs are delivered through a patchwork of school-based, nonschool-based, and home-based providers of varying quality. While often disjointed and difficult to navigate, the diversity of settings sometimes has at least one important Strength: In a democratic society, the provision of services could be best shaped by citizen needs and preferences. Parent choice would be strengthened in a more coherent early childhood education system.

Parent Power. It is well established that family engagement is a key component of high-quality early childhood education.[23] As early as the 1970s, Head Start parents were granted authority for program budgets and personnel. Head Start parents were viewed as having two important capabilities: to make intelligent decisions and to advocate on behalf of their children. Today, well beyond the Head Start community, family engagement is fully established as key to successful early childhood education.[24]

PRESERVING OUR STRENGTHS: CAUTIONS

We certainly recognize that the intangibles and soft skills we articulate are ideals not fully actualized by all early childhood educators and programs at all times. Nevertheless, we believe that they do represent the character, aspirations, values, and uniqueness of our field. These intangibles represent the field's Strengths—dividends our field has earned over a long period of time.

Efforts to professionalize the early childhood education field must avoid the paradigm that learning all we can about a specific profession (hard skills) is *the sole* pathway to success. Of course, hard skills are important. But hard skills alone do not account for the intangibles that early childhood educators must develop to achieve significant progress with children and their families. Chief among our soft skills is partnership with and respect for the parent voice; being a "professional" must never diminish our appreciation for the role of families.

Never underestimate the value of soft skills! Never undervalue the Strength that early childhood education has already demonstrated in these areas. The "minors" (the intangibles) are essential to achieve the "majors" (child outcomes).

As professional mastery emerges, the spotlight on hard skills may dim, while soft skills continue to play a large role in determining successful outcomes. All of us have to engage in this precarious blending process. We must keep up with the latest knowledge base and field-wide advances without losing our human edge. There is not an easy answer to this dilemma, and skilled improvisation is required!

How does the professionalization of the field of early childhood education impact these soft skills—the 3% difference that adds power to the profession? How do we grow and build Competence—including preservation of our Strengths and character? What else might we do to face our adaptive challenges?

Early childhood educators must be so much more than their job description. The bottom line is this: The new early childhood professional probably won't get the job interview or the promotion without the required hard skills, but it's the soft skills—the 3%—that will accelerate the educators' effectiveness.

In 2004, the National Scientific Council on the Developing Child summarized the importance of soft skills with this synthesis: "Stated simply, relationships are the 'active ingredients' of the environment's influence on healthy human development."[25]

Reflecting on this idea, in 2017 Junlei Li asks:

> This naturally leads to two practical questions. One, how do we recognize these developmental interactions in everyday settings? Two, how do we help such interactions grow? . . . I wonder if we could create more time and space for "practice-based practice" where we take time to recognize what we have known but taken for granted in everyday practice under a new, appreciative, affirmative light.[26]

Achieving Balance: What We Must Add as We Professionalize

In this chapter, we emphasize the importance of Strengths, preserving the field's 3%, as a Guiding Principle for advancing the field of early childhood education. Below are six areas of focus about Strengths that we "must add" in our efforts to professionalize the field.

1. *Nurture educator commitment by meeting educators' financial needs and making it easier for them to stay in the field.* Although most early childhood educators would like to continue a career in the field for the foreseeable future, many are not at all sure that they will be able to do so.[27] They are not performing these roles solely for compensation, but the lack of sufficient pay and benefits is a significant obstacle for them. Indeed, the early childhood educators with the lowest household incomes are somewhat more likely to expect to pursue other careers.[28]

2. *Cultivate cultural connections using the human capital of the field's diverse workforce.* Unlike K–12 education where there is a dearth of teachers of color,[29] the field of early childhood education has a tremendous and perhaps underutilized asset of workforce diversity.[30] Nevertheless, for decades, a sense of professional isolation and

marginalization has been voiced by professionals of Asian, African, and Latino heritage.[31] In the recent NAEYC survey, educators of color were more likely to perceive a range of obstacles compared with Whites, including finding jobs, affording the cost of a college degree, navigating the process of getting a degree, finding employment that matches their skills, and understanding the various requirements for becoming a teacher. Early childhood educators of color also express more concern than do Whites about opportunities for mentoring and training.[32]

In addition to cultivating cultural connections with the field's diverse staff, there is an ongoing need to cultivate connections with the diverse families we serve. For example, we know that family engagement, child socialization, and parenting techniques may differ by race, by parental educational attainment, by socioeconomic status, and by parents' language.[33]

> Children only have one childhood. We can't do it over. Zero to Three says we have a powerful and professional duty to do the best for our children. We need teachers who have the full complement of education and skills, and who are nurturing and passionate.
>
> —Belinda Rojas from Texas

Yet, the reality is that most early childhood educators receive little to no training in appropriate family engagement practices and often lack the necessary skills and competencies needed to address a range of family, cultural, linguistic, and religious backgrounds.[34]

3. ***Lower language barriers because the profession's change strategies cannot leave important assets (people) out.*** Given the field's focus on degree attainment, it is worth noting that 80% of immigrant early childhood educators are employed in home- or family-based settings, suggesting that they may be isolated from many professional development opportunities. Although practitioners who are English language learners are interacting with children every day, many professional development opportunities require English proficiency, thereby limiting opportunity for both the practitioner and the children served.

Career pathways for English language learners in early childhood education are particularly daunting since those practitioners begin the journey with both lower incomes and less educational attainment than native-born peers (nearly 20% lack a high school diploma; nearly one-half live below 200% of the federal poverty line, compared with less than 25% of native-born early childhood educators).

Successful support strategies have been demonstrated, but are not widely available.[35] The Council for Professional Recognition makes a commitment to support these practitioners by offering the CDA

PROFILE OF MARTA ROSA, MTR CONSULTING SERVICES IN MASSACHUSETTS

"Despite all the research that's been conducted on the value of quality early care and education programs, there is still little political will to provide families the support they need to afford it," says Marta T. Rosa, who has worked in the early childhood education field in a variety of roles.

"We know early childhood education works. We know it's the right pathway to success in life," she says. "We just don't want to invest in it as a society. There are still many people that see this as a parenting issue and not a societal good."

Society believes public education is an entitlement, but doesn't see early childhood education the same way. That means families continue to patch together the care they can afford, and then when their children are old enough for public preschool or kindergarten, they move on to other concerns. The business sector, she says, also has not made support for families with children a high priority.

"Excellent care costs. It is going to take government and employers and corporations working together to meet the needs of parents," she says. "I don't see advocacy flourishing for this."

Rosa worked directly in the early childhood education field for many years and served as the president of the National Association of Child Care Resource and Referral Agencies before it became Child Care Aware. She was the first Latina to be elected to public office in Chelsea, Massachusetts, and served on both the school committee and the city council. More recently, she served as the chief diversity officer at Wheelock College and also has a consulting business. "My passion is to make this world a better place for children and families. I enjoy taking on projects where I'm sharing ideas, strategies, and the work with other committed professionals," she says.

Diversity within the early childhood workforce is probably its greatest asset, Rosa says, but adds that it hasn't been recognized as a Strength. More immigrants and women of color are working in the field, but they aren't getting the support they need to grow as teachers and to afford higher education. While pilot projects or programs show promise, she says, "we haven't figured out how to marry compensation with competency and knowledge building."

She also sees a "generational divide" between tenured education professors who "haven't stepped into an early childhood education program for the last 20 to 30 years" and young early educators who are unprepared for the policies and the realities of today's classrooms. "Higher education owns a piece of this," she says, "because they have not kept up with this generation."

assessment in any language that is being used in their practice with young children, opening doors for English language learners.

4. ***Advocate for a mixed delivery system.***[36] One major concern for efforts to professionalize the field is that the financial pressures on nonschool options already have led to the closure or reduced capacity of private programs, thereby reducing parental choice. These outcomes are viewed as undermining the value and feasibility of strong mixed delivery systems and are being challenged. A mixed delivery system recognizes the reality that, for many parents (67%), child-care options are limited, especially for families without strong finances (79%), relative to families with strong financial resources (63%).[37]

   A mixed delivery system has many advantages. Chief among them is the significant experience that these systems have in delivering services to children and their families. The community spaces that they represent allow states or communities to more rapidly expand their classrooms—while reducing the taxpayer burden to create new locations.

   Most important, mixed delivery systems effectively meet the needs of working families who require full-day, full-year early childhood education services. In addition to the convenience of a single location, mixed delivery systems also provide greater continuity for children.

   Given the tremendous growth of state-funded pre-K programs, it is notable that most states use a mixed delivery system that may include public schools, Head Start grantees, and private child-care centers.[38] Because a mixed delivery system has been a Strength of the field, we must work to preserve and strengthen family options.

5. ***Promote parent power and partnerships, not asymmetrical hierarchies.*** Relationships with families are a field-wide value where the ideals seem to exceed the realities. For example, QRIS,[39] now active in at least 38 states, strongly encourages the inclusion of family engagement through metrics on communication, program governance, and collaborative learning initiatives.[40]

   Nevertheless, few states' QRIS include standards that describe explicit requirements for programs to help parents learn about ways they can promote their children's learning. For example, in its policy brief,[41] the Pew Center on the States reported that only about half of state-funded prekindergarten programs, now operating in 41 states, require parent engagement activities.

   Some observers have credited this exclusion of family engagement by the field, in part, to the increased demands for program standards and accountability, the move toward expansion of formal child care, and the expectations among policymakers for professionalization of the field.[42]

Critics argue that state universal preschools and private preschool programs have a professional culture that inadvertently "discourage[s] caring and relational family engagement practices,"[43] which agency directors may perceive as unprofessional. "Professionals face pressures that undermine the use of family-centered early childhood education practices, as policy makers expect programs to consolidate decision-making power." In this view, these programs promote a culture of detachment and foster authoritarian behavior rather than professional–family partnerships.

6. ***Focus on results, not structures.*** In the past 10 years, several states have undergone transformations in state organizational structures to best support young children. The New America Foundation[44] reports that while a consolidated approach seems as if it would best be able to manage and align systems, that is not necessarily true, depending on the state's cultural, political, and economic context. In other words, keep an eye on the purposes intended to be achieved and ensure that the systems have an external-facing focus that can communicate clearly about the profession.

Facing Goliath: Affirmations

As the field moves toward greater professionalization, it is important that it decide what is essential to retain and bring forward, and map and preserve its assets. We affirm:

We draw Strength from the early childhood education community.

We are in a beloved community where we don't have to be like everyone else to be supported and cherished. Our community is full of people who value compassion, justice, love, and truth, although we may have different opinions. Our colleagues are full of good will and have good hearts. We encourage and even challenge one another to higher and more ethical living.

In our community, we stay connected!

"We see you!" *Sawubona* is a Zulu greeting that means "I see you."[45] It says, "I see your personality. I see your humanity. I see your dignity and Respect." In a community context where everyone knows everyone else, it's an exceedingly powerful representation of understanding. We in early childhood education see and value our diversity.

We are here!

The response to the Zulu greeting *Sawubona* is *Ngikhona*, which means "I am here." Inherent in the response is the sense that until you saw me, I didn't exist. Furthermore, there is a Zulu proverb, *Umuntu ngumuntu nagabantu*, which means "A person is a person because of other people." The television show *Cheers* expressed it this way: "You want to be where everybody knows your name." Families and colleagues: We know your names and we are here for you.

We are preserving the 3% that matters.

Our intangibles equal our soft skills; our relationships make us strong! The extra 3% makes a significant difference!

Reflect on the Guiding Principle of *Strengths*

The Latina in me is an ember that blazes forever.

—Sonia Sotomayor, lawyer, U.S. Supreme Court justice

1. What embers in your profession are worth preserving forever?
2. Give an example of when you added improvisation to your practice. What happened? How do you reflect on that experience?
3. What is your strongest "soft skill"? How does it make the symbolic 3% difference in your life?
4. Think about the field's culture.
   a. What cultural shifts are emerging?
   b. What aspects of the field's culture are either being developed or gaining Strength? What are your thoughts about these?
   c. What aspects of the field's culture are losing ground? What are your thoughts about these?
   d. What can you do to build on the field's Strengths?

CHAPTER 4

Equity

Equity is a Guiding Principle closely tied to the Principles of Respect, Competence, and Strengths. Clearly researchers of the early childhood education field have extensively studied and documented inequities among children—by race, language, family immigration status, and other forms of diversity. For example, African American children in particular are largely without access to high-quality early childhood education.[1] Further, poor and minority children and children of immigrants continue to attend lower-quality ECE programs at a higher rate than their peers.[2] Poverty decreases access to high-quality early childhood education in terms of affordability, particularly among undocumented families who may not have access to government-subsidized child care.[3]

To what extent—and how—are inequities manifested among early childhood educators? And, what can we do about it? Let's look again at questions about Equity, because we cannot truly professionalize the field without doing so.

WHAT IS EQUITY?

In its most basic sense, Equity is the Principle of being fair and impartial: It is freedom from bias or favoritism. In an equitable society, advantage and disadvantage would not be predictable by race, language, or similar factors. Equity is an ideal condition in which all members of society have basic rights, protections, opportunities, obligations, and social benefits. Defining Equity may seem innocuous, but actualizing Equity is not a simple matter.

Right away we recognize that beyond this simple definition, there are profound complexities. We all have a personal history, and we share a national legacy, about Equity. In many ways, we would all rather not talk about Equity because it reveals discomfort, divergence, anxiety, and uncertainty. What, after all, does "fair" mean?

To join a conversation about Equity is to make a decision to get comfortable with being uncomfortable, to face "Goliath." Yes, it is difficult to talk about issues such as race.[4] But, as Margaret Wheatley tells us, we must be "willing to be disturbed."[5]

REALITY, EQUALITY, AND EQUITY

Let's start by distinguishing the current reality from the concept of equality and the idea of Equity, as illustrated in Figure 4.1.

- The *reality* is that unequal access and opportunity are still pervasive in the United States in almost every area of society, including indicators of health, education, housing, and income.[6] No matter how sincere our intentions, we cannot simply wish away the knotty pain of our national history and become "race neutral" because of the institutionalized policies, procedures, and practices that continue to have disproportionate negative impacts on certain individuals, populations, and communities.[7]
- Then we must consider the vision of *equality*: Although frequently used as synonyms, equality—giving everyone the same thing—is not the same as Equity. Indeed, equality (a sameness, or equal division of assets) may fall short of achieving justice.
- This leads us to the concept of Equity—the recognition that some places and people need to receive a greater investment than others in order to achieve the results that are intended. Equity encompasses a wide variety of strategies that may be considered fair, but not necessarily equal. The concept of Equity is that different treatment, rather than treating everybody the same, is necessary to obtain justice.

Figure 4.1. A Comparative Look at Equality, Equity, and Reality

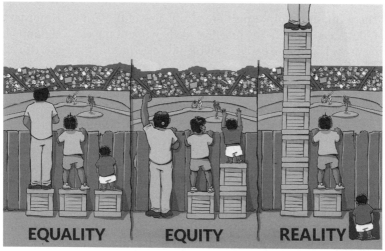

Source: Interaction Institute for Social Change (interactioninstitute.org). Art by Angus Maguire (madewithangus.com), with an adaptation by Andrew Weizman.

The idea of Equity is not always easy to digest. Do we measure Equity by increasing opportunity or should it be measured according to outcomes? Does it mean that some people or groups will have to give up power so that others can have more?[8]

As authors, we talk about Equity as:

- infinite power that we exercise *with* others rather than *over* others
- protection of the human rights of those deprived of them
- an instrument for growth and professional cohesion

IRONIES OF EQUITY

In Chapter 1, we name three major ironies in the field of early childhood education:

1. Although the field has worked to shift thinking about children from a deficit to a Strengths approach, this focus on assets is not always extended to the people who care for and educate young children.
2. Insufficient levels of Respect have been rendered to the professionals who are themselves deeply immersed in gaining Respect for the children and families we serve.
3. The public is now convinced of the value of early childhood education yet tolerates widespread poverty and limited opportunity among the people who provide that education.

These questions of Respect are also issues of disparities. Unmistakable inequities are evident in the practical, daily work of the early childhood educator, as well as in the extent to which these educators can exercise agency over the work. The Goliaths are large and unrelenting: Compensation parity, representative leadership, and opportunities for professional growth are just a few.

EQUAL PAY FOR EQUAL WORK?

Compensation parity for early childhood educators typically is defined as comparable pay with kindergarten and elementary school teachers with similar qualifications.[9] Looking at compensation through an Equity lens, we ask: What are the root causes of compensation inequities? When examining this issue, we find evidence of disparities related to the market economy of child care, as well as the educational penalty often experienced by practitioners in the early childhood education industry.

Economic System Disparities

For the most part, salary parity for early childhood educators remains an aspiration. This is true regardless of the system or setting in which the educator works, or the age group that is served.

The extent of inequity often depends on the program setting and its source of funding. Typically, funding for the 59% of the workforce employed in private center–based settings (not schools, Head Start, or publicly funded preschool) is dependent on parent fees, a weak foundation on which to place heavy burdens of compensation parity.

Preschool teachers tend to make more money when they work for a public school system and in places where the state funds prekindergarten.[10] Yet, even in publicly funded preschools, in all 50 states early childhood educators with the same qualifications earn significantly lower salaries than kindergarten teachers and other elementary school teachers.[11] This inequity persists even when the state requires a bachelor's degree for preschool teachers at state-funded programs.[12]

Without question, a root cause of inequity is the unimpeded market economy that serves as the prevailing source of financial resources for most early childhood education programs. For decades, it has been demonstrated that parents cannot afford to pay the actual cost of the programs. The consequence is that these programs have fewer resources for both the children and the staff.[13] While government subsidies for poor children allow them valuable access to programs, the level of financial support offered to programs from government sources has been abysmally low.[14]

Despite convincing evidence about the inadequacy of market forces to support high-quality early childhood education, government has not acted as a countervailing power or safety net for the protection of the practitioner.[15] By its inaction, government enables or tolerates lower quality and unequal opportunity for the children and families impacted by the deferral gap—the gap between public acclaim and public investment in the field.[16]

Consequently, it stands to reason that if community-based programs dependent on local market conditions (parent fees) are able to hire degreed teachers, they are unable to retain them. If these teachers can move to a publicly financed setting or school, their salaries nearly double.[17]

The Education Penalty

Typically, college graduates have greater success in the labor market than people with no education beyond high school. Their higher levels of employment and higher wages are an "education premium." But there are complexities and variations in the return on the investment in postsecondary education.[18]

Early childhood educators are one of the groups for whom there is widespread uncertainty about the financial return on the higher education investment. The compensation payoff is disappointing when compared with other professions. Wages of child-care workers with a high school degree are 28% lower than those of similarly educated non-child-care workers, while child-care workers with a bachelor's degree have wages 44.8% lower than those of similarly educated non-child-care workers. According to Gould,[19] there are pay increases with educational attainment among child-care and non-child-care workers alike; however, the pay disparities increase as well.

WHY MUST WE FOCUS ON EQUITY?

The entire profession of early childhood education experiences inequity! Both market forces and the education penalty for early childhood educators compound to strain the field's efforts to build a coherent and effective early childhood education system. Changing early childhood educators' qualifications (or other factors) *without* addressing institutionalized inequity is insufficient to change the fundamental asymmetrical power dynamics of our field. These are social justice issues and therefore are an imperative of any efforts to professionalize the field.

In addition, the Albert Shankar Institute report[20] points out that issues of teacher quality and educational opportunity cannot be adequately considered irrespective of student and teacher demographics. Yet issues of race typically are overlooked in teacher training and professional development; there is a lack of educator preparation explicitly focused on race and class.[21]

So, let's be clear: Racial and gender inequities trap the field of early childhood education in a challenging loop. Not addressing these factors impacts who will enter our occupation.[22] Then, low pay makes it difficult to attract and retain more experienced staff with the higher levels of education that are required in order to fulfill the promise of preschool.

To professionalize the field in a sustainable manner, the field must:

- analyze its circumstances through an Equity lens—a systemic framework used to reveal and address disparities[23]
- create strong inclusive networks of the people impacted by inequities—which is all of us
- take action from a social justice stance

NAMING THE ELEPHANT IN THE ROOM

An Equity lens requires us to ask: *Who* is being impacted by policies, procedures, or practice, and *how* are different groups being impacted? Only when we look dispassionately at the "who" and the "how" can we strategically reduce or remove inequities.

Whether we are talking about quality rating systems, degree attainment, compensation, or "who's in" and "who's out," many aspects of our professional work point to the intersectionality of Respect, gender, and race.

- As previously discussed, there is a lack of Respect for early childhood educators, even as the transformative power of the work we perform is recognized. The younger the age of the child served, the less Respect might be accrued to the role of early childhood educator. This is one reason why the wage gap between those who work with infants and toddlers and those who work with preschool-aged children is particularly stark when looking at annual wages.[24]

- Gender matters.[25] Virtually all early childhood educators are women (97%)[26] and working with children is often thought of as "women's work." We can hardly overlook the fact that pay disparity by gender is a well-researched phenomenon that impacts women across professions and across their entire lifetimes.[27] While child-care workers constitute about 1.1% of all workers, 2.3% of all female workers are child-care workers.[28]

  One result of the gender phenomenon is that men in the field often face discrimination. Another result of the gender phenomenon is that more education for women generally,[29] and for early childhood educators specifically, does not close the wage gap.[30] Right now a college degree in early childhood education—a degree earned predominantly by women—has the lowest projected earnings of all college degrees.[31]

  > We've had a situation where parents didn't feel comfortable with one of the teachers in the toddler classroom changing diapers because he was a male. But changing diapers is a normal part of what he does in his professional role. This work is part of a profession—not a gender role.
  >
  > —Kamilah Washington from Massachusetts

- Race and national origin matter. Not only are almost all child-care workers female,[32] but they are also disproportionately workers of color.[33] Child-care workers are predominantly U.S.-born, but, as compared with other workers, are slightly more likely to be foreign-born. Most child-care workers are non-Hispanic White, but are more likely to be non-White or Hispanic than workers in other occupations. Nearly one-fifth (19.8%) of child-care workers are Hispanic (compared with 15.7% of workers in other occupations), and 14.1% of child-care workers are non-Hispanic

Black (compared with 10.6% of workers in other occupations). In other words, child-care workers are more likely to fall into demographic groups that have lower wages on average (e.g., women, immigrants, those with less than a college degree, and racial and ethnic minorities).[34]

Compensation and other opportunity gaps in the early childhood work-force have been documented.

- Ullrich, Hamm, and Herzfeldt-Kamprath reported racial wage disparities in the early childhood workforce.[35] While noting the need for increased compensation for all early childhood educators, they revealed that poor compensation and benefits are felt most acutely by African American women. The wage gap between Black and White females is about 93 cents on the dollar—a meaningful sum for low-wage workers.
- In a 2017 study about the demand for teacher characteristics in the child-care market, Boyd-Swan and Herbst reported several race-related variations.[36] Job applicants with African American– or Hispanic-sounding names were considerably less likely to receive an interview request than otherwise identical White applicants. Relative to White job seekers, the interview rate for African Americans was about 32% lower, and the interview rate for Hispanics was 13% lower.[37] Estimating wages for assistant and lead teachers, Boyd-Swan and Herbst found that female and Black lead teachers earn less than their male and White peers, while Hispanic assistant teachers earn more.[38] Bertrand and Mullainathan state that

  While one may have expected that improved credentials may alleviate employers' fear that African-American applicants are deficient in some unobservable skills, this is not the case in our data. Discrimination there-fore appears to bite twice, making it harder not only for African-Americans to find a job but also to improve their employability.[39]

Let's be clear: Low-wage early childhood education workers are es-sential contributors to our economy. They are critical players in keep-ing our economy humming but are not benefiting from the prosperity they are helping to create. This is inequity—and it is inequity with racial disparities.

REPRESENT!

There is no question that the field of early childhood education has a very strong focus on issues concerning diversity as it relates to children and families. We authors often wonder why issues of practitioners' race and gender are not frequently and explicitly addressed, since these issues clearly impact the field's capacity to achieve compensation equity and eliminate the education penalty.

The field is relatively uninvolved in advocacy efforts involving civic issues not specific to early childhood. These issues include support for raising the minimum wage, securing immigrant rights, advancing women's

---

PROFILE OF B. B. OTERO
PRESIDENT, OTERO STRATEGY GROUP

When B. B. Otero founded CentroNía, a child and family center, more than 30 years ago, she saw the CDA credential not only as a way to educate providers, but also as a way for low-income, immigrant women in Washington, DC, to enter the job market.

"It became a means to helping many immigrant women move beyond domestic work and either start their own business as family child-care providers or be employed in a child-care center where they would achieve job stability and receive benefits," says Otero. "What was paramount to many of the women we worked with was economic stability and a means to support their families."

Since that time, she has seen numerous Latina and African immigrant women earn a CDA, open their own centers or family child-care homes, and even get full-time jobs with benefits in the DC public schools. The CDA program, she adds, also gave these parents "good grounding" as parents, even if they didn't move into the field.

Otero left CentroNía in 2011 to serve as deputy mayor for health and human services, where she oversaw policy and operations for 10 city agencies in the District of Columbia. She oversaw the development of the Early Head Start Child Care Partnership grant, which created hubs across the city providing comprehensive services and training to multiple child development centers seeking to meet Early Head Start standards. Today, she runs a consulting organization that provides issue advocacy, strategic planning, and government relations work.

Knowledge of child development has grown considerably since B. B. began working in the field, and although she is a proponent of early childhood teachers earning college degrees, she believes in the power of experience. "I know the amount of effort, patience, and energy that being in the classroom day in and day out requires," she says. "Older experienced providers who may be unlikely to go back to school can be important mentors and coaches for younger teachers, particularly in working with families."

equality, and urging community justice. Yet, these are issues that impact large numbers of early childhood educators on a daily basis. An Equity lens requires us to stand in solidarity as voices for the protection of the human rights of our colleagues who may be deprived of them.

However, within the early childhood education arena, there are countless examples of successful advocacy efforts among early childhood educators. These efforts have resulted in very significant infusions of public dollars that have supported professional development and degree acquisition, and subsequently led to higher quality programs with less turnover.[40] Applying the lessons learned from these successes to partnerships with relevant social justice issues could be productive.

SPEAK!

The concept of representative leadership, a vital component of Equity, simply states that the voices of practitioners must be heard, engaged, empowered, and reflected in any planning, decisionmaking, or evaluations about them. "Nothing about us without us" is a strategic imperative. Representative leadership is an expression of infinite power that we exercise *with* others rather than *over* others.

An Equity lens asks us to examine *who* is speaking for the field of early childhood education and *how* the voices of different groups are represented. To what extent are the voices of practitioners meaningfully engaged in the planning, decisionmaking, and evaluation that support efforts to professionalize the field? Engagement of diverse voices will ensure that the field's messages are authentic and representative.

But this notion too often is put to the test when practitioners are considered "consumers" of edicts and regulations rather than empowered and respected partners. Contrast this perspective with values expressed by groups such as the Work Family Resource Center (www.workfamilyresource.org/diversity-in-leadership-alliance), a child-care resources and referral agency in North Carolina that, as part of its commitment to racial Equity and diversity, states that leaders and advocates are needed who more closely reflect the cultural, racial, ethnic, and linguistic diversity of the children and families served by the early childhood education system.[41]

In many ways, the field of early childhood education is doing well on matters of diversity. Impressively:

- The field has a longstanding focus on issues of diversity and inclusion for children and families.[42]
- The early childhood education workforce is more representative of the children it serves than the K–12 teaching force. Only 18% of K–12 teachers identify as a race other than non-Hispanic White.

By contrast, people of color account for nearly 40% of the total early childhood education workforce, a much closer representation of the children of color served (44%).[43] Only 7% of public school teachers are Black—and just 2% are Black men.[44] A report about K–12 education from the Education Trust reports that non-White teachers are exiting the profession at higher rates than their White counterparts, reporting that they felt their expertise and professional contributions were dismissed or unnoticed.[45] Yet research on the K–12 education system shows that teachers of color are linked to improved student outcomes and increased self-esteem of students of color because they serve as models of professional success.[46]

Nevertheless, practitioners of color consistently indicate that the field falls short of representative leadership.[47]

- There are demographic differences between the field's "leaders" and actual early childhood education teaching staff. An Equity lens invites us to be curious about any organization where leadership roles are filled predominantly by White persons and representation of people of color is in lower levels of the organization.
- Several researchers have found that racial and ethnic diversity tends to decline as credential requirements increase.[48]
- Whitebook and her colleagues[49] found in their study that, across job levels, ethnic diversity decreased as job-level responsibility increased, with the category of director showing the least amount of diversity. Less than one-quarter (24%) of directors and less than one-half of supervisors/managers (42%) were non-White, whereas more than one-half of professional (55%) and administrative (59%) staff were non-White. Moreover, agency directors emerged as the least linguistically diverse group, and administrative staff as the most linguistically diverse.

As the demographics of the field continue to change, the concept of representation also must change to include new voices and strategies. For example, translation services or shifting cultural norms may become essential as new groups are more predominantly included in the field.[50]

INEQUITIES HAVE CONSEQUENCES

Disparities have consequences. One most unfortunate consequence is the impact of disparities on the well-being of individuals or groups. For example, powerlessness can be experienced when practitioners do not regularly and meaningfully participate in making decisions that affect their working lives. The data are quite clear that early childhood educators lack ideal working conditions, may have little or no autonomy around work tasks, cannot exercise their creativity or judgment fully, and overall do not command Respect, as compared with others.[51] A sense of powerlessness is likely to impact the quality of early childhood education experiences offered to young children, as well as the quality of life for the practitioners themselves.

An Equity lens[52] requires us to ask questions such as:

- Are employment opportunities for individuals distributed in an equitable manner, or do factors such as race benefit some while disadvantaging others?
- How might the profession examine the conditions under which opportunity grows or diminishes as a result of policies, procedures, and practices?
- How might the profession take action to promote or rectify inequities that result from policies, procedures, and practices?

One of the bright lights in the Equity conversation is the extent to which numerous initiatives have supported staff development. Chief among them are the T.E.A.C.H. and WAGE$ programs[53] in 23 states and the District of Columbia, which provide financial and coaching support for early childhood educators to earn credentials and degrees.[54] A disproportionate number of scholarship recipients are people of color, first-generation college students, and low-wage earners.[55] Most inspiring about T.E.A.C.H. and WAGE$ is that these initiatives demonstrate the impact of strategic, collective action and responsibility in holding institutions and systems accountable.

Very positive initiatives also may have unintended consequences that create or accelerate inequities. For example, the Federal Title I funding under the Elementary and Secondary Education Act is designed to enhance and support high-quality pre-K programs, including strengthening and developing the workforce with respect to diversity initiatives. However, public school systems with pre-K programs benefit the most from these funds, and this could contribute to concerns about the strength of the field's mixed delivery system.

Critics claim that expansive government preschool initiatives crowd out private preschool and child-care providers. This can occur in two ways: (1) by limiting private participation with numerous new rules and regulations, and (2) by forcing private providers to compete with "free" taxpayer-funded programs.[56]

A review of the rapid expansion of QRIS reveals that those standards have been largely silent on the question of workforce diversity and the

**PROFILE OF AISHA RAY,
PROFESSOR EMERITUS, ERIKSON INSTITUTE, ILLINOIS**

Attending de facto segregated schools in Chicago and growing up in a family committed to challenging racial and social injustice, Aisha Ray focuses her work on how to reduce educational inequities for children of color, significantly improve the quality of professional development the early childhood workforce receives, and attract leadership, in classrooms and at policy tables, committed to racial Equity.

Top-level conversations about improving early childhood program quality and preparing teachers, she says, tend to suggest that all children, regardless of racial, ethnic, and cultural differences, need the same type of early learning experience and providers with the same knowledge and skills. To an extent this is true—children of color and children in poverty are as capable as any other group of children of creative and critical thinking and acting. The challenge is that the field generally lacks a deep understanding of the normative development of Black, Brown, and Native American children. Our perceptions of these children and their families often are clouded by unexamined deficit views of them as "impoverished," "at risk," and other terms that do not offer enlightenment regarding who they are, what they can do, and how capable they are.

"I don't think there has been the kind of deep conversations in the field about what the education of Black children (or Mexican American, or Navajo children) should involve," says Ray. And "we have not sufficiently and effectively brought into our conversations the perspectives and leadership of scholars and practitioners of color to inform and deepen our understanding. Despite asserting that teachers, administrators, researchers, and others understand the complexity of culture as *the* contextual feature of development, "we do not train teachers to actually know what to do about culture except in the most superficial ways."

Ray was on her way to getting a doctorate in history when she "took a detour" and became a teaching assistant in a Head Start program. She then worked as a practicum instructor at a community college; she later joined the Erikson Institute faculty where she has led a variety of research projects on race, culture, and Equity in early childhood.

She adds that developing a more diverse workforce is not only about White people in the field better understanding Black people, but also about Black, Latino, and Asian people understanding one another. "Everybody needs to get better at working with people who are different from themselves," she says.

While leaders in the field acknowledge that these gaps exist, she thinks many people are still deeply uncomfortable talking about race. That's why she's focusing on developing leaders who can bring a racial and cultural perspective to the state policy arena.

With support from the W.K. Kellogg Foundation and as part of her work with the BUILD Initiative, Ray is co-leading the Equity Leaders Action Network, a diverse group of 34 early childhood professionals working in 20 states. Over a 3-year period, the participants will work to promote more equitable early childhood systems.

"I don't think you can get significant advantages and change for kids of color," Ray says, "unless you can begin to change who is in the pipeline and provides the leadership to make policy."

role diversity plays in the development and delivery of *high-quality* service to young children.[57] It was reported that only 18 of the 40 QRIS programs operating in 38 states across the country include any program indicators related to linguistic or cultural diversity.[58] Here are two examples of this challenge:

- During the debates over Wisconsin's new child-care quality improvement initiative, the YoungStar quality rating system, an anticipated trade-off for quality improvement was likely to be a reduction in the number of child-care providers and a disparate impact on African American child-care providers in Milwaukee.[59]
- Testimony provided to the Oregon Early Learning Council by the Albina Early Head Start program[60] indicated that even though the Albina program had always been highly rated using Head Start standards, it did not score well on the QRIS ratings. The QRIS standards were not in alignment with the Head Start standards. Albina argued successfully that QRIS failed to recognize the importance the program placed on the diversity of staff and its impact on the overall quality of the programs.

These examples illustrate that professionalization efforts, even well-intended ones, can have unintended consequences when they do not take Equity issues into account.

POSSIBILITIES

Having spent a decade working in Massachusetts, we have many examples of the benefits of an Equity lens from that state. As we review some examples, keep in mind that questions, opportunities, and struggles that occur in Massachusetts are likely to be comparable to those in other states. These five examples demonstrate what can be accomplished when an Equity lens and proactive leadership combine to address challenging circumstances.

Example 1: Near the beginning of the universal prekindergarten program in Massachusetts, the system was developed with state funds in a way that did not require recipients to serve children receiving subsidies. As a result, analysis of grant awards revealed that "winners" were communities with populations that were relatively White and wealthy, and served by high-performing programs. But there are solutions when one uses an Equity lens and acts with intention. When Sherri Killins was commissioner of the Massachusetts Department of Early Education and Care (from 2009 to 2013), she shifted the program so that grantees needed to include more children with subsidies. The result was that programs in ethnic-minority, low-income, and special-needs communities received more resources in an attempt to compensate for and overcome pre-existing factors that might have placed them at a disadvantage. Again "equal resource allocation" may not be "equitable."

Example 2: Listening to communities and partnering with them, Commissioner Killins devised a new strategy, using American Recovery and Reinvestment Act[61] funds, which allowed grantees that did not meet all criteria to have "exceptions" that they would remediate within a given period of time. There is recognition among many advocates that in order to participate in QRIS, financial resources are needed in order to make improvements. Without the resources, certain communities would be unable to meet criteria, perpetuating inequity.[62]

Example 3: Noticing that grant funds were not being awarded in rural areas, Commissioner Killins established a special grant that focused on those geographic communities. Furthermore, a stronger rural focus was incorporated into all grants.

Example 4: Many communities required smaller grants in order to get started; writing proposals to the state—given governmental requirements—was a barrier. So, Commissioner Killins collaborated with the United Way, an agency experienced in designing and implementing grant review processes for organizations with limited capacity.

Example 5: In the context of both new and ongoing initiatives, data continue to show that women of color are more likely to be in instructional roles, and Whites are more likely to be in supervisory roles. We authors and many of our colleagues can tell many stories about organizations that insisted that they could not identify any persons of color for managerial positions. In one case Sherri Killins reviewed the position description to discover that the requirements included certifications in ECERS[63] and in the CLASS assessment systems. Simply changing the requirements to indicate that the new employee must *become* certified within a certain period of time, with organizational financial support, enabled the group to expand and diversify its pool of potential hires, and to remove institutional barriers to Equity.

WE MUST ACTIVELY REJECT INEQUITY

The examples cited above demonstrate the importance of active reflection and action to combat inequities. We must understand inequity in our field as part of larger conversations, such as the growing income inequality in the United States. These inequities are due to not only the lack of people of color in higher-paying leadership roles but also the low pay in predominantly female, diverse, community-based programs serving infants and toddlers, for example.

For the most part, it is still women who choose historically female-predominant occupations, such as teaching young children. An Equity lens asks: While it is imperative that women have the opportunity to enter any occupation they desire, how do we value and reward the work being done in early childhood education as equally important as other occupations? Since a large proportion of women and people of color work in this occupation, increasing the level of pay among early childhood educators certainly will contribute to closing gender or racial wage gaps and reducing income inequality.

Some policy analysts, policymakers, and scholars argue that low-wage workers should "work their way out of poverty" by acquiring the human capital that would enable them to leave poverty-level jobs. In a study of immigrant workers by the Center for Poverty Research, affiliates Vicki Smith and Brian Halpin find that "while many of these low-wage workers recognize the need to enhance their skills and educational credentials, the conditions of their employment trap them, making it nearly impossible to escape."[64]

These low-income early childhood educators are working—yet they are still poor, often relying on public assistance to help them to survive.[65] As a result, taxpayers are providing not only support to the poor but also, in effect, a huge subsidy for employers of low-wage workers.

Inequities such as poor compensation, under-representation, and limited opportunity are central to the realities of the field of early childhood education. These realities perpetuate poverty, discrimination, racial and gender bias, and lack of agency by our workforce—hardly a proud foundation on which to build a profession.

We believe that the ethics of the early childhood education field include a duty to reject these symptoms of social injustice and asymmetrical power. Starting points to reject inequity include a duty to:

- recognize our responsibility to promote Equity for the workforce—just as the field has admirably advocated for children and families
- understand how Equity for our profession is related to issues of gender and racial injustice
- ensure that our colleagues have access to the information, resources, and opportunities they need to meaningfully participate in decisionmaking about the course of their lives and careers
- create conditions that encourage Respect for the early childhood educator, including demonstrations of Respect for difference and cultural Competence
- prevent and eliminate exploitation of our colleagues through asymmetrical power and discrimination

WILLING TO BE DISTURBED

The road to Equity is covered in asymmetrical dilemmas that will tax even the strongest among us. Our country, our profession, and each of us are caught in a vise that can make discussions about Equity difficult and painful. To face issues of Equity, we must be "willing to be disturbed." We must be able to understand that the challenges of the field are not, at their core, about individual deficiencies or lack of degree attainment—they are issues of gender, race, language, national origin, and funding.

We also must be willing to acknowledge and confront professional hierarchies that can suppress voices and limit representative leadership. Even within our low-status occupation, there are hierarchies of opportunity shaped by dominant societal values, attitudes, and beliefs. These hierarchies create situations in which a disproportionate share of assets, resources, and positive social value accrues to people and programs by race, by sector, by first language, as well as by other factors.[66] An Equity lens helps us to explore and challenge the consequences of hierarchy, and reinforces the importance of representative engagement.[67]

When it comes to questions of Equity, many people despair. They feel that Equity is unattainable. How will we know what steps to take in the right direction? It's hard to work toward an ideal society even if you think you know what it is. Amartya Sen suggests that we don't think of social justice in terms of an ideal society.[68] Instead, think of it in terms of clear specific injustices that can be reduced or addressed by opportunities to participate, to have your voice heard, or to earn a livable wage.

Achieving Balance: What We Must Add as We Professionalize

In this chapter, we emphasize the importance of Equity as a Guiding Principle for advancing the field of early childhood education. Here are seven areas of focus on Equity that we "must add" in efforts to professionalize the field.

1. Make Equity an everyday priority. We must make Equity an ongoing priority of the professionalization agenda and be willing to work for change. We will "cast down our buckets where we are,"[69] explore our everyday challenges, and prepare ourselves mentally, politically, and economically to work for Equity.
2. Adopt an Equity lens whenever we face a challenge, an opportunity, or a change strategy. We must confront concerns that doing so will have a negative impact on program quality.[70] Using an Equity lens requires respectful discussion and commitment to democratic processes, which require engagement of many voices. We protect the human rights of *both* child and adult populations that historically have suffered discrimination. For our field, an Equity lens can be an instrument for growth and professional cohesion.[71]
3. Address racial and gender inequality explicitly but not necessarily exclusively. We will ask: Who is impacted by the action? Then we will engage affected communities. We intentionally include perspectives from multiple paradigms. We recognize when viewpoints from the dominant paradigm are privileged.
4. Focus on impacts rather than intentions. We will know that good intentions are necessary but not sufficient to achieve Equity.
5. Emphasize structural and institutional Equity rather than only personal prejudice or professional deficiencies. We make a commitment to examine inequities in our profession and in our institutional structures. We will ask: What are the root causes?
6. Support social justice issues whenever they impact our professional community. This means that we will work with other professions and groups to reduce or eliminate:
   » income inequality
   » racism and discrimination
   » gender bias
   » exploitation and disparities of power that keep too many people in our workforce impoverished

7. As Marilyn Cochran-Smith[72] suggests, actively address the dynamics of oppression and privilege. We do this by engaging in self-reflection and learning about these issues. The field of early childhood education does not exist in a vacuum separate from the broad society that has historically rooted, institutionally sanctioned stratification along socially constructed group lines that include race, class, gender, language, and ability (among others).

Facing Goliath: Affirmations

As the field moves toward greater professionalization, it is important that we address disparities, exercise power with others, protect the rights of our colleagues, and serve as an instrument for professional cohesion. We affirm:

We share power with others.

We share the sentiments expressed by Lilla Watson, inaugural president of the Aboriginal and Islander Child Care Agency in Australia: "If you have come to save me, you are wasting your time. But if you have come because somehow your liberation is wrapped up in mine, then let us work together."

We are willing to be disturbed. (Thank you, Margaret Wheatley.)

We reckon with our history. We are doing all that we can do where we are right now. We advance by being proactive in our present situations. We now do every day all that can be done that day.

Today we do what we want to see tomorrow.

We let future priorities have an influence on today's activities. We have the power to make our actions successful. We put the whole power of our faith and purpose behind our actions. Our progress is rapid and clear. When it is time to act, we act with courage, certainty, and confidence.

We grow in unity with all people.

We have infinite power that we exercise *with* others. We protect the rights of anyone deprived of them whether we are affected or not.

Reflect on the Guiding Principle of *Equity*

Justice will not be served until those who are unaffected are as outraged as those who are.

—Benjamin Franklin, scientist, diplomat

1. What do the terms *Equity* and *social justice* mean to you?
2. In this chapter, several examples from the Commonwealth of Massachusetts were offered to demonstrate the possibility of field-wide change when one looks at circumstances through an Equity lens.
   a. Name examples of inequity in your state or local polices, practices, or procedures.
   b. Name examples of inequities that have been overcome in your state or local policies, practices, or procedures.
3. Think about a specific issue of Equity that matters to you.
   a. How does it impact everyday life for yourself or people you care about?
   b. What are symptoms of asymmetrical power in this issue?
   c. What actions could be taken to confront this inequity?
   d. Whom can you encourage to work on this issue with you?
   e. What is the result you want to achieve?

CHAPTER 5

Synthesis

Elevate, Unite, Claim Power—Let's Go!

The Guiding Principles we have articulated here—Respect, Competence, Strengths, and Equity—are foundations that anchor our aspirations for the field of early childhood education. These Guiding Principles support quality professional practice for individuals, for systems, and for policies. Using these Guiding Principles, we continually ask ourselves: Are we doing the right thing for our profession and the people who work in it?

The critical principles of Respect, Competence, Strengths, and Equity are of significant importance for the well-being of young children for reasons that include the rapidity of early brain development,[1] high parental employment,[2] and scientific consensus about the power of high-quality teaching for children in the early years.[3]

So, how can we best proceed to advance our profession, to support the workforce, and to serve young children well? Generations of early childhood educators would recognize that there is an "aspiration gap"[4] between the Guiding Principles and our national realities. To close this aspiration gap, we consider an insight offered by Matthew Taylor, chief executive of the Royal Society of Arts: "A better future demands a more resourceful population. In terms of the economy, this means a workforce which is more entrepreneurial, creative and flexible. . . . [A] core objective of public policy must be to help people align current behaviours with future challenges and hopes."[5] Given Taylor's insight, we believe that now is the time when we as an occupational community of practice must take "big bets"[6] on social and societal change for our profession, for our children, and for ourselves—change that will require both early childhood educators and public policy to be more resourceful. We suggest three strategies: First, we must elevate the voice of the early childhood educator; second, we must unify using Guiding Principles; and third, we must claim power through effective public policy.

> **THE EARLY CHILDHOOD EDUCATION PROFESSION TODAY**
>
> Early childhood educators are people whose profession is highly valued, of deferred value, and undervalued all at once!

ELEVATE OUR VOICES: NEXT STEPS

What can we do now? We offer the following four ideas as critically important "next steps" the field must take to elevate the voices of early childhood
educators.

First: ***Strengthen public awareness of the reciprocal and immutable connection between the status of the early childhood educators and the well-
being of the children they teach.*** We must help families and policymakers
understand that paying early childhood educators poverty wages and asking them to function at a high level in suboptimal working conditions is a
disservice to everyone.[7] Indeed, any hesitancy to highlight and meaningfully address workforce issues must be overcome for the sake of the children.
Inaction and neglect of these issues can have dire consequences for our
children and for the early childhood education field of practice.

- We notice that press reports about mandates to increase staff
  qualifications have been followed immediately by family objections
  to the impact of these changes on the cost of their child care. From
  these concerns about cost, dozens of online comments express
  disrespect for the work, with commenters asking: Why do "day care"
  workers need degrees anyway? How hard can the work really be?[8]
- Families who pay for early learning services seem largely unaware
  that their fees, although a substantial part of the family budget, are
  hardly adequate to pay the cost of high-quality care.[9]
- And the larger policy question speaks to the profession's broader
  call for public investment: Should children receive a quality of
  services that is only as good as their parents can afford?
- While abundant early learning improvement efforts focus
  on administrative structures, curriculum, or assessment,[10]
  sustainable change can occur only in proportion to the number
  of early childhood educators ready to create the conditions for
  success needed to move the initiatives forward with excellence.
  Implementation science is beginning to give more recognition to
  the notion that improving student outcomes through evidence-
  based programs requires engaging the hearts and minds of
  educators.[11]

Second: ***Emphasize the perspectives of the people who provide direct
services to children and families through this profession.*** We advance our
profession when we listen to the lived experience of practitioners and
deepen opportunities for their participation in change strategies. To best
understand the connection between the professional workforce and a
child's well-being, we must trust and value the early educators' training,

competencies, and experiences. We begin by asking early educators: What do you think? How do you feel? What do you need? Conversely, we must hear them when they emphasize that they are part of the process and solution. "Nothing about us without us"[12] is a statement that supports their desire for inclusion.

This desire speaks to the importance of participatory democracy, where there is broad constituent involvement in any change effort. This leads to the third next step.

Third: *Name the field's challenges for what they really are—institutionalized oppression.*[13] Oppression is injustice. It is the "abuse" of authority, law, funding, custom, or force to create or sustain inequities. Unfortunately, these inequities are ubiquitous among those of us in early childhood education. They can be surreptitious too—often remaining unnamed, ignored, or explicitly denied in efforts to professionalize the field.

The *Oxford English Dictionary* defines *oppression* as "the state of being subject to unjust treatment or control." Some classic forms of oppression are racism, sexism, and class bias. Because these forms of systemic oppression often occur as points of "intersectionality," they do not function independently of one another, but overlap with various social identities that are interconnected and interactive.

This means that while the entire field of early childhood education may face oppression as a whole, some people in the field may experience oppression differently than others, with additional social identities and intersections such as race or language.

Oppression leads to asymmetrical conflicts that have real-life consequences for individuals (losing a job or opportunities for advancement); for groups (race/class disparities); as well as for the profession as a whole (the education penalty or the deferral gap). While any individual situation may not be based solely on race, gender, first language, or social class, these factors (alone and in intersection with one another) are among the most egregious disparities evident in the field both historically and now.

To constructively confront personal biases, poverty among our colleagues, and asymmetrical privilege takes courage and skill. Experiencing occupational oppression can be painful for the staff to share—and painful for allies to hear. Debates about the "hierarchies of oppression"[14] in teacher education only demonstrate the difficulty of having conversations about oppression.

Enormous sensitivity is required, including work to address responses generally characterized as "White fragility": "a state in which even a minimum amount of racial stress becomes intolerable, triggering a range of defensive moves. These moves include the outward display of emotions such as anger, fear, and guilt, and behaviors such as argumentation, silence, and leaving the stress-inducing situation."[15]

Fourth: ***Consciously consider how our plight is linked to other forms of institutional oppression that may occur in different contexts, and support efforts that seek to diminish them.*** The children we serve—and we ourselves—are impacted by issues such as immigration, misogyny, and community violence. We cannot view these issues as "other" or regard them as if the professionalization of our field can occur outside of these considerations.[16] As Audre Lorde reminded us, "Your silence will not protect you." To elevate the voices of early childhood educators requires an incontrovertible commitment to advocating for multiple forms of diversity (e.g., age, ethnicity, and gender) and Equity in every teaching, administrative, or policy setting. We cannot change what we cannot face.

UNIFY WITH SYSTEMS THINKING: NEXT STEP

If we cannot end now our differences, at least we can help make the world safe for diversity.

—John F. Kennedy, Commencement Address at
American University, June 10, 1963

Because the four Guiding Principles are precepts to direct, encourage, influence, and support our professional intentions and change strategies over time, they can effectively serve as a unifying factor among us. ***The next best step for the field is to increase its understanding of and its appreciation and capacity for "systems thinking" as the Guiding Principles are applied to strategic actions.***

Why We Highlight Systems Thinking

Systems thinking is a high-priority focus for the field of early childhood education because our work is clearly awash in system failures and fragmentation. Evidence of system failures is abundant:

- For decades, the field has had a fluctuating sense of its purpose, identity, and responsibilities.
- Fragmentation and rivalries among sectors of the field are normative.
- A hierarchical pecking order among us values various roles in the field differently (e.g., being an infant teacher relative to being a kindergarten teacher).
- Occupational allegiances are framed by the age of the children served, the funding source, or the program's auspice (e.g., "I work in Head Start").

- The field's delivery mechanisms are chaotic, uncoordinated, and of uneven quality.

In sum, the field's work is compartmentalized into competing parts that individually and collectively undermine attention to the whole.[17] The inevitable conclusion from the evidence at hand is that our current ways of being are inadequate to the needs of children, families, and the workforce. If we accept this assertion, we also must conclude that even the most expert adjustments to the current system will fail to produce fundamental, transformative, or sustainable change in the core issues we face. In an occupation growing ever more complicated, crowded, and interdependent, resolution of any of the field's challenges cannot be achieved by fixing one piece in isolation from the others.[18]

A critical next step for early childhood education is the creation of deeper levels of synergy; the actions we take must emerge from the perspective that the whole network of early childhood education is greater than the sum of its parts. We must function more effectively as a collaborative whole to achieve a common purpose. A systems approach recognizes our interconnectivity and that our fate is shared.

In *The Fifth Discipline* by Peter Senge, systems thinking is defined as "a discipline for seeing wholes." According to Senge,

> It is a framework for seeing interrelationships rather than things—for seeing patterns of change rather than static "snapshots." It is a set of general principles—distilled over the course of the twentieth century, spanning fields as diverse as the physical and social sciences, engineering, and management. . . . And systems thinking is a sensibility—for the subtle interconnectedness that gives living systems their unique character.[19]

Systems thinking provides a framework for seeing dynamic interrelationships rather than system components; patterns of change rather than events; and the structures that underlie complex situations. From this perspective, we strengthen our recognition that individuals and organizations are participants in a larger scheme rather than individual entities reacting to disparate outside forces.[20] In this way, we more clearly notice that the issues of the early childhood education profession are so dynamic and complex that our circumstances now require an emphasis on integrating and uniting as a profession.

Responses to System Failure

We therefore must ask ourselves what kind of system is needed to produce the breakthrough achievements we are seeking. To address this question, it's important to note that the past decade has witnessed dynamic activity as states and localities have worked for improvements through the creation of quality rating systems, career frameworks, and other mechanisms. In some instances, these efforts in themselves have resulted in additional fragmentation for the field, as each state or program has designed its own standards, workforce registries, staff qualification requirements, administrative structures, credentials, and other variables. Insufficient financial resources have been a key barrier to widespread or sustainable change.

Consequently, despite the evidence of accelerating activity across the United States, the diffusion of important, yet isolated, efforts has meant that the early childhood education field has not—and likely cannot through current approaches—develop as a coherent professional system.

Current Initiatives

A professional field of practice requires coherent standards that are established by the profession itself (not via an array of governmental agencies or political processes). We must unify the profession across state boundaries. Fortunately, there are a number of current initiatives that are working to create unity among us. The NAEYC-facilitated Power to the Profession initiative is a collaborative of 15 national organizations that seek to define the field's identity, purpose, and competencies.[21] The National Academy of Sciences is convening a national group of leaders to think about unifying the profession.[22] The National Governors Association[23] and the National League of Cities[24] are both working with constituent groups to develop and implement place-based solutions.

As the important work of these groups progresses, we hope that national standards and frameworks will emerge, including policy proposals that can be presented to the states and that will align government activities with the field's leadership. Proactive communication strategies will be crucial to keep the focus on system building and avoid unintended messaging that can have a fragmenting effect. Revisiting our efforts from a systems-thinking perspective may help us to achieve breakthroughs and to find more effective, more sustainable solutions.

Avoiding and Managing Unintended Consequences

The prior discussion on degree attainment illustrates the need to navigate an array of potential unintended consequences as initiatives for broader system building occur. Jacqueline Jones, president of the Foundation for Child Development, has stated clearly[25] that "earn a bachelor's degree" was never intended to be the "headline" of the 706-page report, *Transforming the Workforce for Children Birth Through Age 8: A Unifying Foundation.*[26] Without question, the report clearly articulates that excellence in early childhood

education requires an intersecting system that includes compensation, a professionally agreed-upon set of competencies, the work environment and working conditions, informed leadership, access to ongoing professional development, and financing of the early childhood education system.

This example is a cautionary tale about the search for "silver bullets," the folly of mumpsimus, and the barriers imposed by self-limiting perspectives. The futurist Joel Barker put it this way in defining "paradigm paralysis": "Whatever our current level of success, we accept it as 'normal' and so continue with the activities, actions, and behaviors that keep us at that point."[27]

Moreover, the solitary headline "earn a bachelor's degree" represents the field's persistence in treating early childhood education as what Bánáthy[28] classifies as a "unitary," rather than a "pluralistic," system with many—sometimes conflicting—goals. We cannot persist in viewing early childhood education as a type of "mechanical system" requiring little feedback from the environment to function; it is an organic system and very complex, with many variables, which require a great deal of feedback.[29]

We are convinced that greater attention to thinking about the field as a collection of interactive, interdependent systems is of vital importance for early childhood education in the 21st century. In sum, we must not "reduce" or interpret current experience using old models and metaphors that are no longer appropriate or useful.

CLAIM POWER THROUGH PUBLIC POLICY: NEXT STEPS

The persistent challenges in our field frustrate all of us at times. We are delighted by greater public attention, yet distressed by the public backlash we sometimes encounter.[30] Access to child care for children is still inequitable, staff salaries are still subpar, and higher education is still out of reach. When we experience frustration, it seems that no matter what efforts are pursued, the circumstances for our field persist—or even worsen—despite the best-intentioned approaches.

Too often the policy domain focuses on the "segmented" parts of the challenge without due attention to the impact each segment may have on other parts of the profession. But we know better. We can't segment or separate degrees from competencies. We can't create the mandate for credentials without compensation considerations. We can't effectively recognize the promise of preschool without recognizing and respecting the workforce. Credentials, compensation, and workforce issues must all work together as part of the early childhood education field. Isolating any of these parts, or behaving as if any of these segments can work alone, creates imbalance and instability and weakens the power of the profession.

Influencing public policy decisions will be an important next step for the field—a step clearly recognized by current initiatives. For example, the NAEYC-facilitated Power to the Profession initiative aims to *first establish a shared framework* of career pathways, knowledge and competencies, qualifications, standards, and compensation *that unifies the entire profession, then work to develop a comprehensive policy and financing strategy* for the systemic adoption and implementation of the framework across states and other jurisdictions.

We believe this Power to the Profession strategy to be a sophisticated and wise systems approach to change. It could be a game-changer. It is not an example of what Albert Einstein called the definition of insanity: doing something over and over again and expecting *a different* result. This approach recognizes that no person, no government, and no single organization can do this work for the field. As early childhood educators, we must now push ourselves to clarify our values, face hard realities, and seize new possibilities. This will be very challenging work!

LEADERSHIP WITHOUT AUTHORITY

The work of Power to the Profession and other current initiatives is work that we assume under our own authority as a profession—not as a government commission or a public task force. Each of us, in today's world, is called to exercise what Heifetz calls "leadership without authority."[31] Heifetz says that while we usually focus attention at the head of the table, leadership may emerge more often from the foot of the table.

Indeed, it may be early childhood educators' very lack of formal authority that will facilitate our capacity to address deep-seated adaptive challenges in order to eliminate the disparities between the values and circumstances we see in the early childhood education, for our children's sake and for ourselves. By this work, we address the "aspiration gap." Indeed, the gap between vision and reality is the place where each of us has the opportunity to lead!

Simply stated, as we add power to our profession, we stand for something that has a visible and tangible impact on us as well as strong potential to influence public policies. We must claim power through public policy because embedding our professional vision into the fabric of the nation's policies is an important part of the professionalization of the early childhood education field. In partnership with government policies and professional leadership, we create coherent and sustainable systems that will impact:

- our ability to serve young children fully and well
- our capacity to advance as a profession
- our nation's economic future

GUIDING PRINCIPLES TO PROFESSIONAL POWER

Respect

We acknowledge and demonstrate absolute dignity for everyone in the field of early childhood education.

We affirm:
We are worthy of Respect!
Our contributions matter—a lot!
We have a safe and productive work environment.
We are economically secure.

Competence

We define the observable and measurable behaviors or characteristics that articulate the field's distinctive contributions.

We affirm:
We are growing in knowledge, experience, and expertise.
We teach others as we learn.
We are able and highly competent.
We always do our best!

Strengths

We decide what is essential to retain and bring forward, and map and preserve its assets.

We affirm:
We draw Strength from the early childhood community.
In our community, we stay connected!
"We see you!" "*We* are here!"
We are preserving the 3% that matters.

Equity

We address disparities, exercise power with others, protect the rights of our colleagues, and serve as an instrument for professional cohesion.

We affirm:
We share power with others.
We are willing to be disturbed.
Today we do what we want to see tomorrow.
We grow in unity with all people.

Remember, professionalizing the field of early childhood education is adaptive work.[32] Therefore:

- There are no pre-existing answers.
- We must face and resolve conflicting values.
- We will need to make tough choices.
- We can expect setbacks and loss as we work toward success.

The inevitability of setbacks and loss is one reason we must be very clear about our Guiding Principles, and especially our Strengths, so that we know what is worth preserving and what will help close our aspiration gap.

And as we move forward, the "elephant in the room" is the need for adequate funding to initiate, sustain, and evaluate change. The unpredictable, disjointed, uncoordinated patchwork of funding at both the state and federal levels is insufficient to accomplish the policy parameters that must be established.

Of course, local communities, states, and our nation are starting, and must start, somewhere that is less than "perfect"—and *so must we as a profession begin with the imperfect position in which we find ourselves.* Ready or not, it is time for the field itself to come together to perform the adaptive work that can be done only by us.

ELEVATE, UNITE, CLAIM POWER!

Using these Guiding Principles, we can face realities. These principles empower us as we embody the courage of our convictions so that we no longer fear taboos that are universal features of social systems (men changing diapers?)[33] or refuse to grapple with them. When everyone knows there are "elephants in the room" (disrespect for the child-care worker?), we find ways to name them, so that they do not remain or become "undiscussables."[34]

Change for the field—and the people who work in it—is not optional. And, as we change we must ensure that:

- Respect for early childhood education practitioners predominates. Our profession will thrive only to the level of esteem in which we hold those who care for and teach young children.
- Core competencies define what we must know and be able to do. Moreover, we are a profession of continuous learners with great capacity for self-reference, self-correction, self-organization, and self-renewal.
- The field's Strengths, and what we want to preserve, anchor the changes for which we are willing to work. We address constant

change creatively, maintaining the ability to both adapt to new environments and transform the environments around us.

- Equity is a priority consideration in everything we do. Because actions and policies deemed to be "race neutral" never are.

Guiding Principles empower us in ambiguous situations. We act, and are not passively acted upon. We lead, and are not merely led. We change as a result of individual choices, not threat of mandates. We know that there are powerful interconnected systems that impact our profession. We strive to strengthen local, state, and national policy options that can better serve the best interests of children, the needs of families, and the well-being of our workforce.

As we indicated in *The New Early Childhood Professional*,[35] the responsibility to work for change belongs to each of us and all of us. Each of us has the capacity to start conversations within the programs in which we work, with the families we serve, and with the public as we encounter it in our daily lives.

We no longer can consider the asymmetrical dilemmas of our field to be unfortunate realities of the choice to work with young children and their families. Rather we must call out opportunity and deferral gaps—and own the right to change courses. We must acknowledge inequity and take action to redress it.

The choice is ours. Using Guiding Principles, let us elevate our voices, unite as one profession, and claim the power that strengthens our work on behalf of children and families.

Let's go!

Notes

Introduction

1. Washington, Gadson, & Amel, 2015
2. IOM & NRC, 2015
3. National Survey of Early Childhood Education Project Team, 2013
4. Organisation for Economic Co-operation and Development (OECD), 2012; U.S. Department of Education, 2015
5. Nores & Barnett, 2014; U.S. Department of Education, 2015
6. IOM & NRC, 2015
7. Garcia, Heckman, Leaf, & Prados, 2016
8. Phillips et al., 2017
9. All references to the story of David and Goliath are adapted from 1 Samuel 17:1–58 (New International Version).
10. Chris Argyris coined the term *undiscussables* in his 1990 book, *Overcoming Organizational Defense*.
11. For example, Whitebook and McLean (2017) state that nowadays "compensation parity is perceived as an achievable policy goal rather than a lofty ideal" (p. 1).
12. There are at least two national collaboratives underway in 2017: (1) Power to the Profession, facilitated by NAEYC (www.naeyc.org/profession/overview) and (2) a natonal workgroup organized by the National Academy of Medicine. See Adams et al., 2017.
13. Herzenberg, Price, & Bradley, 2005
14. S.M.R. Covey, 2008

Chapter 1

1. NAEYC, 2011
2. Kant, 1785/1996
3. Porath, 2014
4. Porath & Erez, 2009
5. Dillon, 2016
6. Shier, 2001
7. NAEYC, 2015
8. Baker, Sciarra, & Farrie, 2016; in 2017 a national study entitled "Financing Early Care and Education with a Highly Qualified Workforce" is being conducted by an ad hoc committee under the auspices of the National Academies of Sciences, Engineering, and Medicine. The vision is outlined in the report *Transform-*

ing the Workforce for Children Birth Through Age 8. See sites.nationalacademies.org/DBASSE/BCYF/Finance_ECE/index.htm.

9. Wolfe, 2015

10. Dichter, Austin, & Kipnis, 2014, p. 78

11. Whitebook, McLean, & Austin, 2016, p. 42

12. Whitebook et al., 2016, pp. 1–2

13. Sutcher, Darling-Hammond, & Carver, 2016

14. Goldstein, 2014; Strauss, 2015

15. U.S. Department of Education, Office of Planning, Evaluation and Policy Development, Policy and Program Studies Service, 2016

16. Ludden, 2016

17. Child Care Services Association, 2015

18. Whitebook, Schaack, Kipnis, Austin, & Sakai, 2013, p. 42

19. V. Washington, 2015

20. Whitebook et al., 2013, p. 17

21. Porath, 2014

22. Schwartz & Porath, 2014

23. V. Washington, 2013

24. Mongeau, 2013

25. NAEYC, 2015

26. IOM & NRC, 2015, p. 4

27. IOM & NRC, 2015, p. 16; see also Auger et al., 2014; Pianta, Barnett, Burchinal, & Thornburg, 2009; Pianta, Downer, & Hamre, 2016.

28. NRC & IOM, 2000, p. 390

29. Whitebook et al., 2014, p. 79

30. Bronson, 2015

31. Fullan & Hargreaves, 2012

32. Fullan & Hargreaves, 2012, p. 30

33. Fullan & Hargreaves, 2012, p. 30

34. Whitebook et al., 2016, p. 6

35. *Education Week*, 2015

Chapter 2

1. Hershbein & Kearney, 2014; IOM & NRC, 2015

2. Whitebook, Austin, Ryan, Kipnis, Almaraz, & Sakai, 2012

3. Bornfreund, Cook, Lieberman, & Loewenberg, 2015

4. V. Washington, 2008

5. Boyd-Swan & Herbst, 2017, found that approximately 60% of lead teachers have less than a bachelor's degree.

6. Bowman, Donovan, & Burns, 2000; NRC, 2008; Zaslow, Tout, Halle, Whittaker, & Lavelle, 2010

7. Manning, Garvis, Fleming, & Wong, 2017

8. National Survey of Early Childhood Education Project Team, 2013; see also Bassok, Fitzpatrick, Loeb, & Paglayan, 2013. This study reported that in 2010, nearly 40% of the ECE workforce had at most a high school degree and a third of the workforce had some college but no bachelor's degree. In 2009, the average ECE worker earned an annual income of $16,215 and an hourly wage of $11.70, and only 28% of workers received a pension and/or health benefits from their employer.

9. Goffin, 2013

10. Bornfreund et al., 2015

11. Campos, 2015

12. Baum, 2014

13. Rasmussen, Northrup, & Colson, 2017

14. Gallup & Lumina Foundation, 2014

15. Weise & Christensen, 2014

16. V. Washington, 2008

17. Whitebook et al., 2012, p. 6

18. U.S. Government Accountability Office, 2012

19. Auguste, Kihn, & Miller, 2010; Fullan & Hargreaves, 2012; Lankford, Loeb, McEachin, Miller, & Wyckoff, 2014; OECD, 2000. There was a well-documented decline in the relative academic ability of teachers through the 1990s. However, an analysis of 25 years of data on the academic ability of teachers in New York State shows a steady increase in the academic ability of both individuals certified and those entering teaching.

20. National Council on Teacher Quality, 2010

21. National Council on Teacher Quality, 2010

22. Embry, 2010; National Council on Teacher Quality, 2001, 2016

23. Whitebook & Ryan, 2011; Zaslow et al., 2010

24. Bornfreund et al., 2015

25. IOM & NRC, 2015

26. IOM & NRC, 2015

27. Kelley & Camilli, 2007; Whitebook & Ryan, 2011; Zaslow et al., 2010

28. National Council on Teacher Quality, 2010, 2016

29. Nadworny, 2016; Whitebook et al., 2014

30. See Barnett & Kasmin, 2017. Whitebook & McLean, 2017, define compensation parity as "parity for salary and benefits for equivalent levels of education and experience, adjusted to reflect differences in hours of work in private settings, and including payment for non-child contact hours (such as paid time for planning)."

31. Leal & EdSource Today, 2017; National Council on Teacher Quality, 2010, 2015

32. Cook, 2015

33. Annie E. Casey Foundation, 2014; National Assessment of Educational Progress, 2015

34. Mongeau, 2016

35. Personal conversation with Jacqueline Jones, U.S. Department of Education

36. IOM & NRC, 2015, p. 7

37. IOM & NRC, 2015

38. Goffin & Washington, 2007

39. V. Washington, 2008

40. Council of Regional Accrediting Commissions, 2015

41. Maxwell, Lim, & Early, 2006

42. Sumrall et al. 2016

43. Boyd-Swan and Herbst, 2017

44. V. Washington, 2015

45. V. Washington, 2015

46. U.S. Department of Health and Human Services (n.d); see also Rasmussen et al., 2017

47. Thomas, 2012

48. Herbst, 2015, states that median wages, about $9.77 per hour, have been largely stagnant for 3 decades. Gould, 2015, has detailed that child-care workers receive compensation so low that they cannot make ends meet.

49. Whitebook & McLean, 2017

50. Dieter, Voltz, & Epanchin, 2002; Irvine, 2003; Ladson-Billings, 1999; Valdés, 1996

Chapter 3

1. Heifetz, 1994; Heifetz, Grashow, & Linsky, 2009; Heifetz & Linsky, 2002

2. Linsky, 2010

3. S. R. Covey, 2004

4. S. R. Covey, 2011

5. Washington & Andrews, 1998

6. Low, Kalafut, & Cohen, 2002

7. Haden, 2014

8. Colker, 2008

9. NAEYC, 2015

10. Barsdale & O'Neill, 2014

11. Wilson, 2010

12. Adams, 1965; Crosswell & Elliott, 2004; Taris, Van Horn, Schaufeli, & Schreurs, 2003; Van Horn, Schaufeli, & Taris, 2001

13. Higgins, 2015

14. Higgins, 2015, p. 60

15. S. R. Covey, 2004

16. S.M.R. Covey, 2008

17. Austin, Sakai, & Dhamija, 2016; Park, McHugh, Batalova, & Zong, 2015

18. NAEYC, 2001, p. 39

19. NAEYC, 2001, p. 69

20. Washington & Andrews, 1998

21. V. Washington, 2015

22. V. Washington, 2015

23. Ramos, 2014; Smith, Robbins, Stagman, & Mathur, 2013; Zigler & Muenchow, 1992

24. Adair & Barraza, 2014

25. National Scientific Council on the Developing Child, 2004, p. 1

26. Li, 2017, p. 4

27. NAEYC, 2015

28. NAEYC, 2015

29. Ahmad & Boser, 2014; Boser, 2014

30. Whitebook et al., 2016

31. Blackwell, 2003; V. Washington, 2005

32. NAEYC, 2015

33. Jeynes, 2005, 2010

34. Jeynes, 2005, 2010

35. V. Washington, 2015

36. League of Woman Voters, 2015; Stephens, 2014

37. Gould & Cooke, 2015; Harvard T.H. Chan School of Public Health, National Public Radio, & Robert Wood Johnson Foundation, 2016

38. Barnett, Carolan, Fitzgerald, & Squires, 2012

39. QRIS (n.d.); Smith et al., 2013

40. Belway, Duran, & Spielberg, 2014; Bruner, Ray, Wright, & Copeman, 2009; Driskell, 2014; McCormick Center for Early Education Leadership, 2014

41. Start, 2010

42. Douglass, 2011; Snow, 2012

43. Douglass & Gittell, 2012, p. 271

44. Bornfreund et al., 2015

45. Posts from the Path, 2015

Chapter 4

1. Barnett, Carolan, & Johns, 2013

2. Child Trends, 2013; Matthews & Jang, 2007

3. Yoshikawa, 2011

4. Metta, 2015

5. Wheatley, 2002

6. IOM, 2015; Whitebook et al., 2016; Whitebook et al., 2014 chapter 3

7. For example, although many labor economists believe that race matters less than the skills an employee brings, Black job seekers both are offered and accept lower wages than Whites. It is believed that racial discrimination could account for at least a third of the wage gap between Black and White workers. See Fryer, Pager, & Spenkuch, 2011.

8. Primary equity theories can be discerned through the following frameworks: Tilly, 2006; Rawls, 1971; Sen, 2000; and Arneson, 2002.

9. Whitebook et al., 2016

10. U.S. Department of Health and Human Services & Department of Education, 2016

11. U.S. Department of Health and Human Services & Department of Education, 2016

12. U.S. Department of Health and Human Services & Department of Education, 2016

13. Gould & Cooke, 2015; National Public Radio, 2016; Schulte & Durana, 2016

14. Khim, 2015; Washington, Marshall, Robinson, Modigliani, & Rosa, 2006

15. Khim, 2015; Washington et al., 2006

16. Minimal progress has been made on issues of the early childhood workforce, according to Guernsey, Williams, McCann, & Bornfreund, 2014: President Barack Obama pledged a $10 billion investment in ECE that was fulfilled, mostly through a one-time infusion of spending from the fiscal stimulus package of 2009.

17. Baum, 2014

18. Bacolod, 2016

19. Gould, 2015

20. Albert Shanker Institute, 2015

21. Milner, 2015

22. Bacolod, 2016

23. Balajee et al., 2012; Oregon Health Authority, Office of Equity and Inclusion, n.d.

24. Gould, 2015; Whitebook & McLean, 2017

25. See Goldstein, 2014, for a chapter on how teaching became a feminized profession.

26. U.S. Department of Health and Human Services & Department of Education, 2016

27. American Association of University Women, 2017

28. Gould, 2015

29. American Association of University Women, 2017; IOM & NRC, 2015

30. National Survey of Early Childhood Education Project Team, 2013

31. Gould, 2015; Whitebook et al., 2015

32. Gould, 2015

33. Gould, 2015

34. Gould, 2015

35. Ullrich, Hamm, & Herzfeldt-Kamprath, 2016

36. Boyd-Swan & Herbst, 2017

37. Similar studies were conducted by Nunley, Pugh, Romero, & Seals, 2015; Bertrand & Mullainathan, 2004; and Oreopoulos, 2011.

38. Boyd-Swan & Herbst, 2017

39. Bertrand & Mullainathan, 2004

40. Schweinhart, 2013; U.S. Department of Education, Early Learning, n.d., 2015

41. Annie E. Casey Foundation, 2015; Barnett, Jung, Frede, Hustedt, & Howes, 2011; Garcia, 2015; Jiang, Ekono, & Skinner, 2015; Oregon Health Authority, Office of Equity and Inclusion, n.d.; U.S. Department of Commerce, Census Bureau, 2013; Vesely & Ginsberg, 2011; Whitebook, Kipnis, & Bellm, 2008

42. NAEYC, 2001

43. Park et al., 2015

44. See *Education Week*, 2015.

45. Griffin & Tackie, 2016

46. Ahmad & Boser, 2014

47. Park et al., 2015

48. Kashen, Potter, & Stettner, 2016

49. Whitebook et al., 2012

50. V. Washington, 2015

51. Ludden, 2016; Nadworny, 2016; Whitebook et al., 2014

52. Annie E. Casey Foundation, 2015; Oregon Health Authority, Office of Equity and Inclusion, n.d.; Balajee et al., 2012

53. T.E.A.C.H. Early Childhood National Center, 2016

54. The *T.E.A.C.H. Early Childhood® and Child Care Wage$® Annual National Program Report 2015–2016* states that T.E.A.C.H. scholarship recipients were as follows: 46% were people of color or of Hispanic origin; 52% came from families with no college graduates; and 56% began T.E.A.C.H. with only a high school diploma. Diversity of Wage$ participants was as follows: 62% were people of color or of Hispanic origin; 99% were women; and 66% earned less than $12 an hour.

55. T.E.A.C.H. Early Childhood National Center, 2016

56. Burke & Sheffield, 2013

57. For a look at quality rating and improvement systems in our multiethnic society, see Bruner et al., 2009.

58. Kashen et al., 2016

59. Dickman, 2012

60. Lynn, 2016

61. U.S. Department of Housing and Urban Development, American Recovery and Reinvestment Act of 2009

62. Herbst, 2016, found that states' QRIS can alter parental preferences for child care and may increase teacher compensation.

63. Harms, Clifford, & Cryer, 2014

64. Smith & Halpin, 2012

65. Jacobs, Perry, & MacGillvary, 2015

66. Sidanius, Pratto, Van Laar, & Levin, 2004

67. Balajee et al., 2012

68. Sen, 2000

69. This is a phrase coined by African American leader Booker T. Washington on September 18, 1895, before a predominantly White audience at the Cotton States and International Exposition in Atlanta.

70. V. Washington, 2015

71. Equity for Children, 2013

72. Sensoy & DiAngelo, 2009

Chapter 5

1. NRC & IOM, 2000

2. Bureau of Labor Statistics, 2017

3. IOM & NRC, 2015; Phillips et al., 2017

4. Taylor, 2014

5. Taylor, 2014, pp. 311–312

6. Foster, Perreault, Powell, & Addy, 2016

7. Research certainly has demonstrated the impact of staffing on program quality. See IOM & NRC, 2015; Phillips et al., 2017.

8. Chandler, 2017; Miller, 2017

9. Refer to the website of Child Care Aware for their special section on families at childcareaware.org/families/.

10. Analysis of recent funding initiatives has shown an imbalance between structural investments and a focus on staffing issues. See Guernsey et al., 2014.

11. For example, see Blase, Fixsen, Sims, & Ward, 2015.

12. "Nothing about us without us!" is a slogan with origins in Central European political traditions that came into use in disability activism during the 1990s and is now used by many populist movements.

13. For definitions of oppression from *Webster's Third International Dictionary*, the *Social Work Dictionary*, the *Blackwell Dictionary of Sociology*, and other sources, visit www.personal.umich.edu/~mdover/website/Oppression%20Compendium%20and%20Materials/Definitions%20of%20Oppression.pdf.

14. Gorski & Goodman, 2011

15. DiAngelo, 2011, p. 57

16. Bánáthy, 1991, p. 80

17. Goffin & Washington, 2007

18. Meadows & Wright, 2008

19. Senge, 2006, pp. 68–69

20. Senge, 2006; Senge, Smith, Ross, Roberts, & Kleiner, 1994

21. An overview of the Power to the Profession initiative can be found on NAEYC's website at www.naeyc.org/profession/overview.

22. Adams et al., 2017

23. National Governors Association, 2017

24. The National League of Cities has a number of early childhood initiatives. For an overview, visit www.nlc.org/early-childhood-success.

25. Personal conversation

26. IOM & NRC, 2015

27. Barker, 1993

28. Bánáthy 1991, p. 35

29. Leonard, 2008

30. For example, public posts in response to news articles in the *New York Times* and *Washington Post* stirred a wave of dismayed reaction from early childhood educators. See Chandler, 2017; Miller, 2017. To read those posts, see www.nytimes.com/2017/04/07/upshot/do-preschool-teachers-really-need-to-be-college-graduates.html?r=1 and www.washingtonpost.com/local/social-issues/district-among-the-first-in-nation-to-require-child-care-workers-to-get-college-degrees/2017/03/30/d7d59e18-0fe9-11e7-9d5a-a83e627dc120_story.html?utm_term=.c6950b92d47b.

31. Heifetz, 1994; Heifetz & Linsky, 2002

32. Heifetz et al., 2009

33. Schoemaker & Tetlock, 2012

34. See Hammond & Mayfield, 2004.

35. Washington et al., 2015

References

Adair, J. K., & Barraza, A. (2014). *Voices of immigrant parents in preschool settings.* Washington, DC: National Association for the Education of Young Children. Retrieved from www.naeyc.org/yc/article/Voices_of_Immigrant_Parents_Adair

Adams, J. S. (1965). Inequity in social exchange. In L. Berkowitz (Ed.), *Advances in experimental social psychology* (Vol. 2, pp. 267–299). New York, NY: Academic Press.

Adams, D., Bornfreund, L. A., Carinci, J. E., Connors-Tadros, L., Fraga, L. M., Guarino, A., . . . Williams, V. (2017). *A unified foundation to support a highly qualified early childhood workforce* (Discussion paper). Washington, DC: National Academy of Medicine. Retrieved from nam.edu/a-unified-foundation -to-support-a-highly-qualified-earlychildhood-workforce

Ahmad, F. Z., & Boser, U. (2014). *America's leaky pipeline for teachers of color: Getting more teachers of color into the classroom.* Center for American Progress. Retrieved from cdn.americanprogress.org/wp-content/uploads/2014/05 /TeachersOfColor-report.pdf

The Albert Shanker Institute. (2015). *The state of teacher diversity in American education.* Washington, DC: Author.

American Association of University Women. (2017). *The simple truth about the gender pay gap.* Washington, DC: Author. Retrieved from www.aauw.org/aauw _check/pdf_download/show_pdf.php?file=The-Simple-Truth

The Annie E. Casey Foundation. (2014). *Early reading proficiency in the United States.* Retrieved from www.aecf.org/resources/early-reading-proficiency -in-the-united-states/

The Annie E. Casey Foundation. (2015). *Race equity and inclusion action guide: Embracing equity: 7 steps to advance and embed race, equity and inclusion within your organization.* Baltimore, MD: Author. Retrieved from www.aecf.org

Argyris, C. (1990). *Overcoming organizational defenses: Facilitating organizational learning.* New York, NY: Pearson.

Arneson, R. (2002). *The level playing field conception.* Palo Alto, CA: Stanford University.

Auger, A., Farkas, G., Burchinal, M. R., Duncan, G., & Vandell, D. (2014). Preschool center care quality effects on academic achievement: An instrumental variables analysis. *Developmental Psychology, 50*(12), 2559–2571.

Auguste, K., Kihn, P., & Miller, M. (2010). *Closing the talent gap: Attracting and retaining top-third graduates to careers in teaching.* Retrieved from www .mckinseyonsociety.com/downloads/reports/Education/Closing_the_talent _gap.pdf

Austin, L. J. E., Sakai, L., & Dhamija, D. (2016). *2016 Alameda County early care and education workforce study*. Berkeley: Center for the Study of Child Care Employment, University of California, Berkeley.

Bacolod, M. (2016). *Do alternative opportunities matter? The role of female labor markets in the decline of teacher supply and teacher quality, 1940–1990*. Irvine: University of California.

Baker, B. D., Sciarra, D. G., & Farrie, D. (2016). *Is school funding fair? A national report card* (5th ed.). New Brunswick, NJ: Rutgers Graduate School of Education, Education Law Center. Retrieved from drive.google.com/file /d/0BxtYmwryVI00WGExT3EtVGhDclE/view

Balajee, S. S., et al. (2012). Equity and empowerment lens (racial justice focus). Portland, OR: Multnomah County.

Bánáthy, B. H. (1991). *Systems design of education: Journey to create the future*. Englewood Cliffs, NJ.: Educational Technology Publications.

Barker, J. A. (1993). *Paradigms: The business of discovering the future*. New York, NY: HarperCollins.

Barnett, W. S., Carolan, M. E., Fitzgerald, J., & Squires, J. H. (2012). *The state of preschool 2012: State preschool yearbook*. New Brunswick, NJ: National Institute for Early Education Research.

Barnett, W. S., Carolan, M., & Johns, D. (2013). *Equity and excellence: African-American children's access to quality preschool*. Center on Enhancing Early Learning Outcomes and National Institute for Early Education Research, Rutgers University. Retrieved from nieer.org/wp-content/uploads/2014/03 /Equity20and20Excellence20African-American20ChildrenE28099s20Access 20to20Quality20Preschool_0.pdf

Barnett, W. S., Jung, K., Frede, E., Hustedt, J., & Howes, C. (2011). *Effects of eight state prekindergarten programs on early learning*. New Brunswick, NJ: National Institute for Early Education Research.

Barnett, W. S., & Kasmin, R. (2017). *Teacher compensation parity policies and state-funded pre-K programs*. Berkeley: Center for the Study of Child Care Employment, University of California, Berkeley.

Barsdale, S., & O'Neill, O. (2014, January). Employees who feel love perform better. *Harvard Business Review*. Retrieved from hbr.org/2014/01/employees -who-feel-love- perform-better

Bassok, D., Fitzpatrick, M., Loeb, S., & Paglayan, A. S. (2013). *The early childhood care and education workforce from 1990 through 2010: Changing dynamics and persistent concerns*. Retrieved from cepa.stanford.edu/sites/default/files /ChangingECCEDynamics.pdf

Baum, S., (2014, February). *Higher education earnings premium: Value, variation, and trends*. The Urban Institute. Retrieved from www.urban.org/sites/default /files/publication/22316/413033-Higher-Education-Earnings-Premium -Value-Variation-and-Trends.PDF

Belway, S., Duran, M., & Spielberg, L. (2014). *State laws on family engagement in education*. Washington, DC: National Parent Teacher Association.

Bertrand, M., & Mullainathan, S. (2004). Are Emily and Greg more employable than Lakisha and Jamal? A field experiment on labor market discrimination. *American Economic Review, 94*, 991–1013.

Blackwell, A. G. (2003). *Preface*. In D. S. Marsh, M. Hawk, & K. Putnam, *Leadership for policy change: Strengthening communities of color through leadership development*. (p. 2). Washington, DC: PolicyLink.

Blase, K. A., Fixsen, D. L., Sims, B. J., & Ward, C. S. (2015). *Implementation science: Changing hearts, minds, behavior, and systems to improve educational outcomes*. Oakland, CA: The Wing Institute. Retrieved from fpg.unc.edu/sites/fpg .unc.edu/files/resources/reports-and-policy-briefs/2014%20Wing%20 Summit%20KB.pdf

Bornfreund, L., Cook, S., Lieberman, A., & Loewenberg, A. (2015). *From crawling to walking: Ranking states on birth–3rd grade policies that support strong readers*. Washington, DC: New America. Retrieved from www.newamerica.org

Boser, U. (2014). *Teacher diversity revisited: A new state by state analysis*. Center for American Progress. Retrieved from www.americanprogress.org/issues/race /reports/2014/05/04/88962/teacher-diversity-revisited/

Bowman, B. T., Donovan, M. S., & Burns, M. S. (Eds.). (2000). *Eager to learn: Educating our preschoolers*. Washington, DC: National Academies Press.

Boyd-Swan, C., & Herbst, C. M. (2017). *The demand for teacher characteristics in the market for child care: Evidence from a field experiment* (IZA DP No. 10702). Institute of Labor Economics. Retrieved from ftp.iza.org/dp10702.pdf

Bronson, B. (2015). Do we value low-skilled work? *New York Times*. Retrieved from www.nytimes.com/2015/10/01/opinion/do-we-value-low-skilled-work.html

Bruner, C., Ray, A., Wright, M. S., & Copeman, A. (2009). *Quality rating and improvement systems for a multi-ethnic society*. Boston, MA: Build Initiative/Third Sector New England. Retrieved from www.buildinitiative.org

Bureau of Labor Statistics. (2017). Employment characteristics of families summary—2016. Washington, DC: U.S. Department of Labor. Retrieved from www.bls.gov/news.release/famee.nr0.htm

Burke, L., & Sheffield, R. (2013). *Universal preschool's empty promises*. The Heritage Foundation. Retreived from report.heritage.org/bg2773

Campos, P. F. (2015, April 4). The real reason college tuition costs so much. *The New York Times*. Retrieved from www.nytimes.com/2015/04/05/opinion /sunday/the-real-reason-college-tuition-costs-so-much.html

Chandler, M. A. (2017, March 31). D.C. among first in nation to require child-care workers to get college degrees. *The Washington Post*. Retrieved from www.washingtonpost.com/local/social-issues/district-among-the-first-in -nation-to-require-child-care-workers-to-get-college-degrees/2017/03/30 /d7d59e18-0fe9-11e7-9d5a-a83e627dc120_story.html

Child Care Services Association. (2015). *Working in early care and education in North Carolina*. Chapel Hill, NC: Author.

Child Trends. (2013). Parental involvement in schools: Indicators of child and youth well-being. Retrieved from www.childtrends.org/?indicators=parental -involvement-in-schools

Colker, L. J. (2008, March). Twelve characteristics of effective early childhood teachers. *Young Children, 63*(2), 68.

Cook, L. (2015, January 28). U.S. education: Still separate and unequal. *U.S. News and World Report*. Retrieved from www.usnews.com/news/blogs/data -mine/2015/01/28/us-education-still-separate-and-unequal

Council of Regional Accrediting Commissions. (2015). Regional accreditors announce common framework for defining and approving competency-based education programs [Press release]. Retrieved from www.insidehighered .com/sites/default/server_files/files/C-RAC%20CBE%20Statement%20 Press%20Release%206_2.pdf

Covey, S. R. (2008). *The speed of trust: The one thing that changes everything.* New York, NY: Free Press.

Covey, S. R. (2004). *The 7 habits of highly effective people: Powerful lessons in personal change.* New York, NY: Simon & Schuster.

Covey, S. M. R. (2011). *The 3rd alternative.* New York, NY: Simon & Schuster.

Crosswell, L. J., & Elliott, R. G. (2004, November–December). *Committed teachers, passionate teachers: The dimension of passion associated with teacher commitment and engagement.* Paper presented at the AARE 2004 Conference, Melbourne, Australia.

DiAngelo, R. (2011). White fragility. *International Journal of Critical Pedagogy, 3*(3), 54–70.

Dichter, H., Austin, L. J. E., & Kipnis, F. (2014). Policy efforts to improve early childhood teaching jobs. In M. Whitebook, D. Phillips, & C. Howes (Eds.), *Worthy work, still unlivable wages: The early childhood workforce 25 years after the national child care staffing study* (pp. 71–79). Berkeley, CA: Center for the Study of Child Care Employment, University of California, Berkeley.

Dickman, A. (2012, April 25). Should we be concerned about the decline in family child care providers? *Public Policy Forum.* Retreived from publicpolicyforum.org /blog/should-we-be-concerned-about-decline-family-child-care-providers

Dieter, L., Voltz, D., & Epanchin, B. (2002). Report of the Wingspread conference preparing teachers to work with diverse learners. *Teacher Education and Special Education, 25*, 1–10.

Dillon, R. S. (2016, Winter). Respect. In E. N. Zalta (Ed.), *The Stanford encyclopedia of philosophy.* Retrieved from plato.stanford.edu/archives/win2016/entries /respect/

Douglass, A. (2011, Fall). Improving family engagement: The organizational context and its influence on partnering with parents in formal child care settings. *Early Childhood Research & Practice, 13*(2), 1–14.

Douglass, A., & Gittell, J. H. (2012, October). Transforming professionalism: Relational bureaucracy and parent–teacher partnerships in child care settings. *Journal of Early Childhood Research, 10*(3), 267–281.

Driskell, N. (2014). A strong start for family engagement in Massachusetts. *FINE Newsletter (VI)5.* Cambridge, MA: Harvard Family Research Project.

Education Week. (2015, January). Early-childhood education in the U.S.: An analysis. Retrieved from www.edweek.org/ew/qc/2015/early-childhood-education -in-the-us.html

Embry, R. C. (2010, December 19). Master degrees don't produce better teachers. *Baltimore Sun.* Retrieved from articles.baltimoresun.com/2010-12-19/news /bs-ed-masters-degree-20101219_1_maryland-teachers-new-teacher -contract-teacher-compensation

Equity for Children. (2013). *Equity and social justice: A short introduction.* Retrieved from www.equityforchildren.org/wp-content/uploads/2013/07/FinalPaper -EquityandSocialJustice-AnIntroduction-1.pdf

Foster, W., Perreault, G., Powell, A., & Addy, C. (2016, Winter). Making big bets for social change. *Stanford Social Innovation Review*. Retrieved from ssir.org /pdf/Winter_2016_Making_Big_Bets_for_Social_Change.pdf

Fryer, R. G., Pager, D., & Spenkuch, J. L. (2011, September). *Racial disparities in job finding and offered wages* (NBER Working Paper No. w17462). Retrieved from ssrn.com/abstract=1935788

Fullan, H., & Hargreaves, M. (2012, June 5). Reviving teaching with "professional capital." Retrieved from www.edweek.org/ew/articles/2012/06/06 /33hargreaves_ep.h31.html

Gallup, & Lumina Foundation. (2014, February). *The 2013 Lumina study of the American public's opinion on higher education and U.S. business leaders' opinion on higher education: What America needs to know about higher education redesign*. Retrieved from www.luminafoundation.org/files/resources/2013 -gallup-lumina-foundation-report.pdf

Garcia, A. (2015, May 13). *Matching the changing demographics of young children in the early education workforce*. Washington, DC: New America.

Garcia, J. L., Heckman, J. J., Leaf, D. E., & Prados, M. J. (2016). *The life-cycle benefits of an influential early childhood program*. Retrieved from heckmanequation.org /assets/2017/01/abc_comprehensivecba_2016-12-05a_jld.pdf

Goffin, S. (2013). *Early childhood education for a new era: Leading for our profession*. New York, NY: Teachers College Press.

Goffin, S., & Washington, V. (2007). *Ready or not: Leadership choices in early care and education*. New York, NY: Teachers College Press.

Goldstein, D. (2014). *The teacher wars: A history of America's most embattled profession*. New York, NY: Anchor Books.

Gorski, P. C., & Goodman, R. D. (2011). Is there a "hierarchy of oppression" in U.S. multicultural teacher education coursework? *Action in Teacher Education, 33*(5–6), 455–475. Retrieved from www.edchange.org/publications/hierarchy -of-oppression-multicultural-education.pdf

Gould, E. (2015, November). *Child care workers aren't paid enough to make ends meet* (Issue Brief No. 405). Washington, DC: Economic Policy Institute. Retrieved from www.epi.org/files/2015/child-care-workers-final.pdf

Gould, E., & Cooke, T. (2015, October 6). *High quality child care is out of reach for working families*. Washington, DC: Economic Policy Institute. Retrieved from www.epi.org/publication/child-care-affordability/

Griffin, A., & Tackie, H. (2016, November). *Through our eyes: Perspectives and reflections from Black teachers*. Washington, DC: The Education Trust. Retrieved from edtrust.org/resource/eyes-perspectives-reflections-black-teachers/

Guernsey, L., Williams, C. P., McCann, C., & Bornfreund, L. (2014). *Subprime learning: Early education in America since the great recession*. Washington, DC: New America. Retrieved from www.newamerica.org/education-policy/policy -papers/subprime-learning/

Haden, J. (2014, April 15). 15 revealing signs you genuinely love what you do: See where you stand—and whether you need to start making changes. Retrieved from www.inc.com/jeff-haden/15-revealing-signs-you-genuinely -love-what-you-do.html

Hammond, S. A., & Mayfield, A. B. (2004). *Naming elephants: How to surface undiscussables for greater organizational success*. Bend, OR: Thinbook Publishing.

Harms, T., Clifford, R., & Cryer, D. (2014). *Environment rating scales: Assessment instruments for early childhood and child care policy* (3rd ed.). New York, NY: Teachers College Press.

Harvard T. H. Chan School of Public Health, National Public Radio, & Robert Wood Johnson Foundation. (2016). *Child care and health in America.* Retrieved from www.rwjf.org/content/dam/farm/reports/surveys_and_polls/2016/rwjf432066

Heifetz, R. A. (1994). *Leadership without easy answers.* Cambridge, MA: Belknap Press, Harvard University Press.

Heifetz, R. A., Grashow, A., & Linsky, M. (2009). *The practice of adaptive leadership: Tools and tactics for changing your organization and the world.* Cambridge, MA: Harvard Business Review Press.

Heifetz, R. A., & Linsky, M. (2002). *Leadership on the line: Staying alive through the dangers of leading.* Cambridge, MA: Harvard Business Review Press.

Herbst, C. M. (2015). *The rising cost of child care in the United States: A reassessment of the evidence* (IZA Discussion Paper No. 9072). Bonn, Germany: Institute of Labor Economics.

Herbst, C. M. (2016). *The impact of quality rating and improvement systems on families' child care choices and the supply of child care labor* (IZA Discussion Paper No. 10383). Bonn, Germany: Institute of Labor Economics.

Hershbein, B., & Kearney, M. (2014, September). *Major decisions: What graduates earn over their lifetimes.* Washington, DC: The Hamilton Project. Retrieved from www.hamiltonproject.org/papers/major_decisions_what_graduates_earn _over_their_lifetimes/

Herzenberg, S., Price, M., & Bradley, D. (2005). *Losing ground in early childhood education: Declining workforce qualifications in an expanding industry, 1979–2004.* Washington, DC: Economic Policy Institute. Retrieved from www.epi.org /publication/study_ece_summary/

Higgins, C. (2015) Why we need a virtue ethics of teaching. In R. Heilbronn & L. Foreman-Peck (Eds.), *Philosophical perspectives on teacher education* (pp. 57–65). West Sussex, England: Wiley.

Institute of Medicine (IOM) & National Research Council (NRC). (2015). *Transforming the workforce for children birth through age 8: A unifying foundation.* Washington, DC: National Academies Press.

Irvine, J. J. (2003). *Educating teachers for diversity: Seeing with a cultural eye.* New York, NY: Teachers College Press.

Jacobs, K., Perry, I., & MacGillvary, J. (2015). *The high public cost of low wages.* Center for Labor Research and Education, University of California, Berkeley Labor Center.

Jeynes, W. H. (2005). A meta-analysis of the relation of parental involvement to urban elementary school student academic achievement. *Urban Education, 40*(3), 237–269.

Jeynes, W. H. (2010). Parental involvement and encouraging that involvement: Implications for school-based programs. *Teachers College Record, 112*(3), 747–774.

Jiang, Y., Ekono, M., & Skinner, C. (2015). *Basic facts about low-income children: Children under 6 years, 2013.* New York, NY: National Center for Children in Poverty, Mailman School of Public Health, Columbia University.

Kant, I. (1996). Groundwork of the metaphysics of morals. In M. Gregor (Trans. & Ed.), *Immanuel Kant practical philosophy* (pp. 37–109). New York, NY: Cambridge University Press. (Original work published 1785)

Kashen, J., Potter, H., & Stettner, A. (2016). *Quality jobs, quality child care: The case of a well-paid, diverse early education workforce*. New York, NY: The Century Foundation.

Kelley, P., & Camilli, G. (2007). *The impact of teacher education on outcomes in center-based early childhood education programs: A meta-analysis*. New Brunswick, NJ: National Institute for Early Education Research.

Khim, S. (2015). Child care isn't just a personal problem. It's an economic one, too. Retrieved from newrepublic.com/article/121797/child-care-isnt-just-personal-problem-its-economic-one-too

Ladson-Billings, G. (1999). Preparing teachers for diverse student populations: A critical race theory perspective. In A. Iran-Nejad & P. D. Pearson (Eds.), *Review of research in education, 24* (pp. 211–247). Washington, DC: American Educational Research Association.

Lankford, H., Loeb, S., McEachin, A., Miller, L. C., & Wyckoff, J. (2014). *Who enters teaching? Encouraging evidence that the status of teaching is improving*. Retrieved from cepa.stanford.edu/sites/default/files/Who%20Enters%20Teaching%20 2014.11.18.pdf

League of Women Voters. (2015). Children and families—Early care and education (Issue paper). Retrieved from www.lwvwa.org/pdfs/2015%20Early%20 Childhood.pdf

Leal, F., & EdSource Today. (2017, February 11). Shortage puts more unqualified teachers in classrooms, survey says. *Los Angeles Daily News*.

Leonard, A. (2008). *Organic (and a little mechanistic) management systems and their application at the public library*. Retrieved from alisonleonardeportfolio.weebly .com/uploads/6/4/1/1/6411965/organic_and_mechanistic_managment _systems.pdf_

Li, J. (2017). Growing simple interactions inside everyday practice. *ALIGN Journal: From Theory to Practice—Residential Care for Children and Youth Special Edition, 3(March)*, 2–6. Retrieved from www.alignab.ca/wp-content/uploads/2017/03 /ALIGN-Journal-March-2017-Revised-From-Theory-to-Practice-Residential -Care-for-Children-and-Youth.pdf

Linsky, M. (2010, September 27). Pushing against the wind. *Faith & Leadership*. Retrieved from www.faithandleadership.com/multimedia/marty-linsky-pushing -against-the-wind

Low, J., Kalafut, P., & Cohen, P. (2002). *Invisible advantage: How intangibles are driving business performance*. Cambridge, MA: Perseus.

Ludden, J. (2016). Poverty wages for U.S. child care workers may be behind high turnover. *MPR News*. Retrieved from www.mprnews.org/story/2016/11/07 /npr-poverty-wages-child-care-workers-turnover_

Lynn, A. (2016, September 27). Oregon Early Learning Council testimony. Retrievable by request from Albina Headstart program: http://www.albinahs .org

Manning, M., Garvis, S., Fleming, C., & Wong, G.T.W. (2017, January). The relationship between teacher qualification and the quality of the early childhood education and care environment. *Campbell Systematic Reviews, 1.* doi:10.4073 /csr.2017.1 ISSN 1891-1803.

Matthews, H., & Jang, D. (2007). *The challenges of change: Learning from the child care and early education experiences of immigrant families.* Center for Law and Social Policy. Retrieved from www.clasp.org/resources-and-publications/publication -1/0356.pdf

Maxwell, K. L., Lim, C-I., & Early, D. M. (2006). *Early childhood teacher preparation programs in the United States: National report.* Chapel Hill: University of North Carolina, FPG Child Development Institute.

McCormick Center for Early Education Leadership. (2014). *The relationship between administrator qualifications and family engagement.* Wheeling, IL: Author.

Meadows, D. H., & Wright, D. (2008). *Thinking in systems: A primer.* White River Junction, VT: Chelsea Green Publishing.

Metta, J. (2015, July 10). I, racist [Blog post]. Retrieved from www.huffingtonpost .com/john-metta/i-racist_b_7770652.html

Miller, C. C. (2017, April 7). Matter of degree: Do preschool teachers really need to be college graduates? *New York Times.* Retrieved from www.nytimes .com/2017/04/07/upshot/do-preschool-teachers-really-need-to-be-college -graduates.html

Milner, M. R., IV. (2015). *Rac(e)ing to class: Confronting poverty and race in schools and classrooms.* Cambridge, MA: Harvard Education Press.

Mongeau, L. (2013). Head Start requirement boosts college degrees for early childhood educators. *EdSource.* Retrieved from edsource.org/2013/head-start -requirement-boosts-college-degrees-for-early-childhood-educators/25375

Mongeau, L. (2016). What Boston preschools get right. *The Atlantic.* Retrieved from www.theatlantic.com/education/archive/2016/08/whatbostons-preschools -get-right/493952/

Nadworny, E. (2016, June). It doesn't pay to be an early-childhood teacher. NPRED. Retrieved from www.npr.org/sections/ed/2016/06/14/481920837 /it-doesnt-pay-to-be-an-early-childhood-teacher_

National Academy of Medicine. (n.d.). Innovation to Incubation (i2l) Program. Retrieved from nam.edu/programs/innovation-to-incubation/

National Assessment of Educational Progress. (2015). *Early reading proficiency: Reading assessment 2015.* Washington, DC: IES National Center for Educational Statistics.

National Association for the Education of Young Children. (2001). NAEYC at 75 (1926–2001): Reflections on the past, challenges for the future. Retrieved from eric.ed.gov/?id=ED463854

National Association for the Education of Young Children. (2011). *Code of ethical conduct and statement of commitment: A position statement of the National Association for the Education of Young Children.* Washington, DC: Author. Retrieved from www.naeyc.org/files/naeyc/image/public_policy/Ethics%20Position%20 Statement2011_09202013update.pdf

National Association for the Education of Young Children. (2015). *Executive summary: Early childhood educators: Advancing the profession.* Retrieved from www .naeyc.org/files/naeyc/Key%20Findings%20Presentation.NAEYC_.pdf

National Council on Teacher Quality. (2001). *Teacher certification reconsidered: Stumbling for Quality.* Retrieved from nctq.org/dmsView/Teacher_Certification _Reconsidered_Stumbling_for_Quality_NCTQ_Report

National Council on Teacher Quality. (2010). *Restructuring teacher pay to reward excellence.* Retrieved from www.nctq.org/dmsView/Restructuring_Teacher_Pay_To_Reward_Excellence_NCTQ_Report

National Council on Teacher Quality. (2015). *2015 state teacher policy yearbook: National summary.* Retrieved from www.nctq.org/dmsView/2015_State_Teacher_Policy_Yearbook_National_Summary_NCTQ_Report

National Council on Teacher Quality. (2016). *Landscapes in teacher prep.* Retrieved from www.nctq.org/dmsView/UE_2016_Landscape_653385_656245

National Governors Association. (2017, February 26). *Early childhood education* (Position paper). Retrieved from www.nga.org/cms/policy-positions/edw/early-childhood-education

National Public Radio. (2016). School money: The cost of opportunity series. Retrieved from www.npr.org/series/473636949/schoolmoney

National Research Council (NRC) & Institute of Medicine (IOM). (2000). *From neurons to neighborhoods: The science of early childhood development.* Washington, DC: National Academy Press.

National Research Council (NRC). (2008). *Early childhood assessment: Why, what, and how.* Washington, DC: National Academies Press. doi.org/10.17226/12446

National Scientific Council on the Developing Child. (2004). *Young children develop in an environment of relationships: Working paper no. 1.* Retrieved from developingchild.harvard.edu/resources/wp1/

National Survey of Early Childhood Education Project Team. (2013). *Number and characteristics of early childhood education (ECE) teachers and caregivers: Initial findings, national survey of early childhood education (NSECE)* (OPRE Report No. 2013-38). Washington, DC: Office of Planning, Research and Evaluation, Administration for Children and Families, U.S. Department of Health and Human Services.

Nores, M., & Barnett, W. S. (2014). *Access to high quality early care and education: Readiness and opportunity gaps in America* (CEELO policy report). New Brunswick, NJ: Center on Enhancing Early Learning Outcomes.

Nunley, J., Pugh, A., Romero, N., & Seals, A. (2015). Racial discrimination in the labor market for recent college graduates: Evidence from a field experiment. *The B.E. Journal of Economic Analysis and Policy, 15,* 1093–1126.

Oregon Health Authority, Office of Equity and Inclusion. (n.d.). Health equity and inclusion program strategies. Retrieved from www.oregon.gov/oha/PH/HEALTHYENVIRONMENTS/CLIMATECHANGE/Documents/Health-Equity-and-Inclusion-strategies.pdf

Oreopoulos, P. (2011). Why do skilled immigrants struggle in the labor market? A field experiment with thirteen thousand resumes. *American Economic Journal: Economic Policy, 3,* 148–171.

Organisation for Economic Co-operation and Development (OECD). (2000). *Early childhood education and care policy in Finland.* Paris, France: OECD Publishing. Retrieved from www.oecd.org/finland/2476019.pdf

Organisation for Economic Co-operation and Development (OECD). (2012). *Education at a glance 2012: OECD indicators.* Paris, France: OECD Publishing. Retrieved from dx.doi.org/10.1787/eag-2012-en

Park, M., McHugh, M., Batalova, J., & Zong, J. (2015). *Immigrant and refugee workers in the early childhood field: Taking a closer look.* Washington, DC: Migration Policy Institute.

Phillips, D. A., Lipsey, M. W., Dodge, K. A., Haskins, R., Bassok, D., Burchinal, M. R., . . . & Weiland, C. (2017). *Puzzling it out: The current state of scientific knowledge on pre-kindergarten effects: A consensus statement.* Washington, DC: Brookings & Duke Center for Child and Family Policy. Retrieved from www .brookings.edu/wp-content/uploads/2017/04/consensus-statement_final.pdf

Pianta, R. C., Barnett, W. S., Burchinal, M., & Thornburg, K. R. (2009). The effects of preschool education: What we know, how public policy is or is not aligned with the evidence base, and what we need to know. *Psychological Science in the Public Interest, 10,* 49–88.

Pianta, R., Downer, J., & Hamre, B. (2016). Quality in early education classrooms: Definitions, gaps, and systems. *The Future of Children, 26,* 119–137.

Porath, C. (2014, November 19). *Half of employees don't feel respected by their bosses. Harvard Business Review.* Retrieved from hbr.org/2014/11/half-of-employees -dont-feel-respected-by-their-bosses

Porath, C. L., & Erez, A. (2009). Overlooked but not untouched: How rudeness reduces onlookers' performance on routine and creative tasks. *Organizational Behavior and Human Decision Processes, 109,* 29–44

Posts from the Path. (2015, January 8). I see you. I see your personality. I see your humanity. I see your dignity and respect. I see you. Retrieved from postsfromthepath.com/authenticity/i-see-you-i-see-your-personality-i-see -your-humanity-i-see-your-dignity-and-Respect-i-see-you

Quality Rating Improvement System. (n.d.). Top ten questions about QRIS. Retrieved from qriscompendium.org/top-ten/question-1/

Ramos, M. (2014). *The strengths of Latina mothers in supporting their children's education: A cultural perspective.* Child Trends Hispanic Institute. Retrieved from www.childtrends.org/publications/the-Strengths-of-Latina-Mothers-in -supporting-their-childrens-education-a-cultural-perspective/

Rasmussen, K., Northrup, P., & Colson, R. (2017). *Handbook of research on competency-based education in university settings.* Hershey, PA: IGI Global.

Rawls, J. (1971). *A theory of justice.* Cambridge, MA: Harvard University Press.

Ruiz, D. M. (1997). *The four agreements: A practical guide to personal freedom.* San Rafael, CA: Amber-Allen Publications.

Schoemaker, P.J.H., & Tetlock, P. E. (2012, Winter). Taboo scenarios: How to think about the unthinkable. *California Management Review, 54*(2), 5–24.

Schulte, B., & Durana, A. (2016, September). *The new America care report.* Washington, DC: New America Foundation. Retrieved from www.newamerica. org/in-depth/care-report/

Schwartz, T., & Porath, C. (2014, June). The power of meeting your employees' needs. *Harvard Business Review.* Retrieved from hbr.org/2014/06/the -power-of-meeting-your-employees-needs

Schweinhart, L. (2013, August 21). Public funding for early childhood education: How it works now and in the future. *SEEN Magazine.* Retrieved from www. seenmagazine.us/Articles/Article-Detail/ArticleId/3241/Public-funding -for-early-childhood-education

Sen, A. (2000). *The idea of justice.* Cambridge, MA: Harvard University Press.

Senge, P. M. (2006). *The fifth discipline: The art & practice of the learning organization.* New York, NY: Crown Business.

Senge, P. M., Smith, B., Ross, R., Roberts, C., & Kleiner, A. (1994). *The fifth discipline fieldbook: Strategies and tools for building a learning organization.* Crown Business.

Sensoy, O., & DiAngelo, R. (2009). Developing social justice literacy: An open letter to our faculty colleagues. *Phi Delta Kappan, 90*(5), 350.

Shier, H. (2001). Pathways to participation: Opening, opportunities and obligations. *Children & Society, 15*(2), 107–117.

Sidanius, J., Pratto, F., Van Laar, C., & Levin, S. (2004). Social dominance theory: Its agenda and method. *Political Psychology, 25,* 6. Retrieved from www.jstor.org/stable/3792281?seq=1#page_scan_tab_contents

Smith, V., & Halpin, B. (2012). *Low-wage work uncertainty often traps low-wage workers.* Center for Poverty Research, University of California, Davis.

Smith, S., Robbins, T., Stagman, S., & Mathur, D. (2013). *Parent engagement from preschool through grade 3: A guide for policymakers.* New York, NY: National Center for Children in Poverty. Retrieved from nccp.org/publications/pdf/text_1084.pdf

Snow, K. (2012). *Research news you can use: Family engagement and early childhood education.* Washington, DC: National Association for the Education of Young Children.

Start, D. R. (2010). *Engaged families, effective pre-K: State policies that bolster student success.* Pew Center on the States. Retrieved from www.pewtrusts.org/~/media/legacy/uploadedfiles/pcs_assets/2010/pknfamilyengagementfinalpdf.pdf

Stephens, S. A. (2014). *Community-level challenges in implementing a mixed delivery prekindergarten system: A brief review of research and field experience.* New York, NY: Center for Children's Initiatives. Retrieved from www.centerforchildrensinitiatives.org/images/2014/FINAL%20SAM%20PAPER%208-7-14.pdf

Strauss, V. (2015, November 20). Why today's college students don't want to be teachers. Washington, DC: *The Washington Post.* Retrieved from www.washingtonpost.com/news/answer-sheet/wp/2015/11/20/why-todays-college-students-dont-want-to-be-teachers/?utm_term=.73b317cb3bf4

Sumrall, T. C., Scott-Little, C., La Paro, K. M., Pianta, R. C., Burchinal, M., Hamre, B., . . . Howes, C. (2016). Student teaching within early childhood teacher preparation programs: An examination of key features across 2- and 4- year institutions. *Early Childhood Education Journal.* Advance online publication. doi:10.1007/s10643-016-0830-x

Sutcher, L., Darling-Hammond, L., & Carver, T. D. (2016). *A coming crisis in teaching? Teacher supply, demand, and shortages in the U.S.* Learning Policy Institute. Retrieved from learningpolicyinstitute.org/product/coming-crisis-teaching

Taris, T. W., Van Horn, J. E., Schaufeli, W. B., & Schreurs, J. G. (2003). Inequity, burnout and psychological withdrawal among teachers: A dynamic exchange model. In *Anxiety, Stress, and Coping, 17*(1), 103–122.

Taylor, M. (2014, November). Closing the aspiration gap. *Reform: UK.* pp. 310–314 Retrieved from www.reform.uk/wp-content/uploads/2014/11/Closing-the-social-aspiration-gap.pdf

T.E.A.C.H. Early Childhood National Center. (2016). *T.E.A.C.H. early childhood® and child care WAGE$® annual national program report 2015–2016: Addressing equity issues in the early childhood workforce education, compensation & career pathways.*

Chapel Hill, SC: T.E.A.C.H. Retrieved from teachecnationalcenter.org/wp
-content/uploads/2016/11/T.E.A.C.H.-and-WAGE-2016-Annual-Program
-Report-e-version.pdf

Thomas, P. L. (2012). What's really wrong with teacher quality and teacher education? Retrieved from www.alternet.org/whats-really-wrong-teacher-quality
-and-teacher-education

Tilly, C. (2006). *Identities, boundaries and social ties.* London, England: Routledge.

Ullrich, R., Hamm, K., & Herzfeldt-Kamprath, R. (2016, August 26). *Underpaid
and unequal: Racial wage disparities in the early childhood workforce.* Washington,
DC: Center for American Progress.

U.S. Department of Commerce, Census Bureau. (2013, October). Current population survey.

U.S. Department of Education, Early Learning. (n.d.). *Key research studies on early learning effectiveness.* Washington, DC: U.S. Department of Education. Retrieved from www.ed.gov/early-learning/research

U.S. Department of Education, Early Learning. (2015). *A matter of equity: Preschool
in America.* Washington, DC: U.S. Department of Education. Retrieved from
www2.ed.gov/documents/early-learning/matter-equity-preschool-america
.pdf

U.S. Department of Education, Office of Planning, Evaluation and Policy Development, Policy and Program Studies Service. (2016). *The state of racial
diversity in the educator workforce.* Washington, DC.: U.S. Department of Education. Retrieved from www2.ed.gov/rschstat/eval/highered/racial-diversity
/state-racial-diversity-workforce.pdf

U.S. Department of Health and Human Services & Department of Education.
(2016, June). *High-quality early learning settings depend on a high-quality workforce: Low compensation undermines quality.* Washington, DC: U.S. Department
of Education. Retrieved from www2.ed.gov/about/inits/ed/earlylearning
/files/ece-low-compensation-undermines-quality-report-2016.pdf

U.S. Department of Health and Human Services (n.d) *Policy statement on early childhood career pathways.* Washington, D.C. Retrieved from: https://www.acf.hhs
.gov/sites/default/files/ecd/career_pathways_policy_final.pdf

U.S. Department of Housing and Urban Development. (n.d.). Community Development Block Grant Program. Retrieved from portal.hud.gov/hudportal
/HUD?src=/program_offices/comm_planning/communitydevelopment
/programs

U.S. Government Accountability Office. (2012). *Early childhood education: HHS and
education are taking steps to improve workforce data and enhance worker quality.*
Washington, DC: Author.

Valdés, G. (1996). *Con respeto: Bridging the distances between culturally diverse families
and schools, an ethnographic portrait.* New York, NY: Teachers College Press.

Van Horn, J. E., Schaufeli, W. B., & Taris, T. W. (2001). Lack of reciprocity among
Dutch teachers: Validation of reciprocity indices and their relation to stress
and well-being. *Work and Stress, 15,* 191–213.

Vesely, C., & Ginsberg, M. (2011). *Exploration of the status of services for immigrant
families in early childhood education programs.* Washington, DC: National Association for the Education of Young Children.

Washington, B. T. (1895). Booker T. Washington delivers the1895 Atlanta compromise speech. Retrieved from historymatters.gmu.edu/d/39

Washington, V. (2005, January). Sharing leadership: A case study of diversity in our profession. *Young Children*, pp. 23–31.

Washington, V. (2008). *Role, relevance, reinvention: Higher education in the field of early care and education.* Boston, MA: Wheelock College. Retrieved from www.cayl.org/wp-content/uploads/2013/05/Role-Relevance-Reinvention_0-1.pdf

Washington, V. (2009). *Needed in School Teaching: A Few Good Men.* Cambridge, MA: The CAYL Institute

Washington, V. (2013, September). CDA 2.0: Supporting people and advancing our field. *Young Children, 68*(4), 68.

Washington, V. (2015, December). *Opening pathways: Strengthening opportunities for early childhood educators who are English language learners.* Boston, MA: The CAYL Institute.

Washington, V., & Andrews, J. D. (Eds.). (1998). *Children of 2010.* Washington, DC: National Association for the Education of Young Children.

Washington, V., Gadson, B., & Amel, K. L. (2015). *The new early childhood professional: A step-by-step guide to overcoming Goliath.* New York, NY: Teachers College Press.

Washington, V., Marshall, N., Robinson, C., Modigliani, K., & Rosa, M. (2006, February 14). *Keeping the promise: A study of the Massachusetts child care voucher system.* Boston, MA: Bessie Tart Wilson Foundation. Retrieved from www.btwic.org/wp-content/uploads/2010/01/MassachusettsChildCareStudyReport.pdf

Weise, M. R., & Christensen, C. M. (2014). *Hire education: Mastery, modularization, and the workforce revolution.* MA: Clayton Christensen Institute for Disruptive Innovation. Retrieved from www.christenseninstitute.org/wp-content/uploads/2014/07/Hire-Education.pdf

Wheatley, M. J. (2002). *Turning to one another: Simple conversations to restore hope to the future.* San Franscisco, CA: Berrett-Koshler. Retrieved from www.ode.state.or.us/opportunities/grants/saelp/willing-to-be-disturbed.pdf

Whitebook, M., Howes, C., & Phillips, D. (1989). The National Child Care Staffing Study: Who cares? Child care teachers and the quality of care in America. Oakland, CA: Child Care Employee Project.

Whitebook, M., Austin, L. J. E., Ryan, S., Kipnis, F., Almaraz, M., & Sakai, L. (2012). *By default or by design? Variations in higher education programs for early care and education teachers and their implications for research methodology, policy, and practice.* Berkeley: Center for the Study of Child Care Employment, University of California, Berkeley. Retrieved from cscce.berkeley.edu/files/2012/ByDefaultOrByDesign_FullReport_2012.pdf

Whitebook, M., Kipnis, F., & Bellm, D. (2008). *Diversity and stratification in California's early childhood education workforce.* Berkeley: Center for the Study of Child Care Employment, University of California, Berkeley. Retrieved from cscce.berkeley.edu/diversity-and-stratification-in-californias-ece-workforce/

Whitebook, M., & McLean, C. (2017). *In pursuit of pre-K parity: A proposed framework for understanding and advancing policy and practice.* Berkeley: Center for the Study of Child Care Employment, University of California, Berkeley.

Whitebook, M., McLean, C., & Austin, L. J. E. (2016). *Early childhood workforce index*. Berkeley, CA: Center for the Study of Child Care Employment, University of California, Berkeley. Retrieved from cscce.berkeley.edu/early-childhood-workforce-index/

Whitebook, M., Phillips, D., & Howes, C. (2014). *Worthy work, still unlivable wages: The early childhood workforce 25 years after the national child care staffing study*. Berkeley,CA: Center for the Study of Child Care Employment, University of California, Berkeley.

Whitebook, M., & Ryan, S. (2011). *Degrees in context: Asking the right questions about preparing skilled and effective teachers of young children* (Preschool Policy Brief Issue 22). National Institute for Early Education Research.

Whitebook, M., Schaack, D., Kipnis, F., Austin, L. J. E., & Sakai, L. (2013). *From aspiration to attainment: Practices that support educational success* (Los Angeles Universal Preschool's Child Development Workforce initiative). Berkeley: Center for the Study of Child Care Employment, University of California, Berkeley.

Wilson, B. (2010). *Love at work: Why passion drives performance in the feelings economy*. Leicester, England: BPS Books.

Wolfe, R. B. (2015). Trends in early childhood education workforce development. In H. Dichter (Ed.), *Rising to the challenge: Building effective systems for young children and families, a BUILD E-book*. Retrieved from buildinitiative.org/Portals/0/Uploads/Documents/E-BookChapter4TrendsInnovationsEarlyChildhood EducationWorkforceDevelopment.pdf

Yoshikawa, H. (2011). *Immigrants raising citizens: Undocumented parents and their children*. New York, NY: Russell Sage Foundation.

Zaslow, M., Tout, K., Halle, T., Whittaker, J. V., & Lavelle, B. (2010). *Toward the identification of features of effective professional development for early childhood educators: Literature review*. Washington, DC: Office of Planning, Evaluation and Policy Development, U.S. Department of Education.

Zigler, E., & Muenchow, S. (1992). *Head Start: The inside story of America's most successful educational experiment*. New York, NY: Basic Books.

Index

Note: Comments contributed by early childhood educators are indicated by *italicized* page numbers.

About the Authors

Valora Washington and Brenda Gadson are coauthors (with Kate Amel) of *The New Early Childhood Professional* (2015, Teachers College Press).

Dr. Valora Washington is chief executive officer of the Council for Professional Recognition and founder of the CAYL Institute in Massachusetts. The Council credentials entry-level early childhood educators who work in preschool, infant/toddler, family child-care, and home visitor settings. Through her work with the Council, she leads the largest credentialing program for early educators in the United States.

She formerly served as vice president at Antioch College and the Kellogg Foundation; as executive director of the Unitarian Universalist Service Committee and of the CAYL Institute; as associate dean at American University; as assistant dean at Howard University; and as a tenured faculty member at the University of North Carolina at Chapel Hill.

Committed to action, research, and policy change, Dr. Washington has coauthored or coedited over 50 publications, including *Children of 2010, Children of 2020, Ready or Not: Leadership Choices in Early Care and Education,* and *The New Early Childhood Professional.* Her advocacy work includes working to change the voucher system in Massachusetts, which gave 52,000 children opportunities for a 1-year certification period. Through the Families for Kids initiative, Dr. Washington designed and coordinated efforts to change the child welfare system in 13 states. This initiative is regarded as a precursor to important legislative changes enacted by President Clinton.

Throughout her career, Dr. Washington has cofounded several organizations, including Voices for Michigan's Children, a statewide advocacy group; the Early Childhood Funders Collaborative; and the CAYL Institute. Frequently tapped for senior-level service, she has been co-chair of the Massachusetts Governor's School Readiness Commission, board chair of Voices for America's Children, secretary of the National Association for the Education of Young Children (NAEYC), chair of the Black Caucus of the Society for Research in Child Development, and co-chair of the National Head Start Association Commission on 2010. She has been a member of numerous task forces and boards, including for the Boston Children's Museum and Wheelock College.

Among many honors, Dr. Washington holds honorary degrees from Urban College, Bennett College, Meadville Lombard Theological School, and Wheelock College. She was selected for the prestigious Barr Fellowship (2009) and Leadership Greater Washington (2013). Dr. Washington has received professional recognition from Boston AEYC; NAEYC Black Caucus; Cambridge Resource and Referral Agency; Center for Adoption Research, University of Massachusetts; National Association of Black Social Workers; United Way of Massachusetts Bay; and others. She was named one of "25 Most Influential Working Mothers" by *Working Mother* magazine in February 1997, and in 1980 she was chosen as one of "Ten Outstanding Young Women of America" from among 62,000 nominations.

Dr. Washington was educated at both Indiana University and Michigan State University. Since 2001, she has been a Certified Association Executive with the American Society of Association Executives.

Brenda Gadson is the principal of BMG Consulting, a firm that specializes in working with community-based non-profits. She has 13 years of experience working within the early childhood education community and has been a lifelong advocate of social justice for children and families.

Brenda has served as executive director, president, or CEO of several non-profit community organizations in Massachusetts, including the Roxbury Multiservice Center. She founded the Boston Center for Community and Justice Inc. and served as the founding executive director for Massachusetts Families for Kids, an adoption- and foster care systems–reform initiative. As owner/operator of BMG Consulting, she is frequently tapped to stabilize, strengthen, and support non-profit organizations in leadership transition and organizational management. Her strengths include strategic planning, project management, leadership and organizational development, program development, executive coaching, and systems analysis work. Brenda has been affiliated with the CAYL Institute as a Program and Management Consultant since 2004. She has also consulted with The Council for Professional Recognition since 2012.